EAST SIDE KRAZY
TRULY MISLEAD

Michael Colyar

LETS PUT THEM GUNS DOWN YOUNG BROTHERS
BEFORE WE END UP IN A MUSEUM...
NEXT TO THE DINOSAURS —
EXTINCT!

EASTSIDE KRAZY - TRULY MISLEAD
Michael Colyar
Post Office Box 44513
Eden Prairie, Minnesota 55344
andrecol18@yahoo.com

ISBN # 978-0-9826466-3-2

Copyright © 2010 by Michael Colyar All rights reserved. Reproduction of text in whole or in part without the express written consent of the author is not permitted and is unlawful according to the 1976 United States Copyright Act.

Cover Designed / Photography by: Vincent Smith

Published by: Heavenly Enterprises Midwest, Ltd.
Chicago, Illinois • 773-783-2981
service@heavenlyenterprises.com

BLESSINGS

First of all, I give honor to GOD, and I also extend a blessing and good health to everyone that reads and takes heed to the message in this book. Make no mistake, the message in which this book is intended is to reveal the grace of GOD, and how GOD can take the foolish things of this world and use them to confuse the wise. My people, don't think it strange when you go through trying and tragic times, 'cause the days we live in are overwhelmingly evil. In these days the hearts of men and women have grown enormously wicked. Selfishness, lovers of money, lovers of sexual pleasures, addicts to drugs and alcohol, friends turning on friends, and ultimately friends killing friends. The Bible speaks of wars and rumors of wars, friends turning on friends, nation rising against nation, children will turn against parents, and parents against children. When I was growing up, I glamorized being a baller, and I wanted respect. I wasn't gonna get played, so I sold drugs and dropped out of school. I held these things to heart.

Now, some of us did become ballers and made money, and some of us have done some terrible things, but there are consequences to these things, and some of us don't get a second chance in our consequences. But guess what? GOD's love for you is so strong that He will forgive you no matter what you have done and no matter what it is. Nothing can separate you from the love of GOD. I have friends that have died to this street life, and friends that have life sentences. The main purpose of this book is to warn you. There are some of you that are on your way to the penitentiary, or the cemetery, or maybe you're in the penitentiary about to come home. We wanna keep you from these places. JESUS said I am the truth, the way, and the life. The truth has all the answers to all your questions. We love you and don't just be a man, but be a man of GOD!!!

Rashad Lewis

TABLE OF CONTENTS

Ain't Know Peace Over East
In The Belly Of The Beast.................... 1

The Dream Team 5

Not Bowing To Bowen 13

Purse First And Ass Last 17

You Gotta Charge It To The Game 21

The Black Steve-O 28

Every Lesson Is Still A Blessing....................... 33

Clubs, Cars, And Big Rap Stars 44

These Girls Are B.D. Angels 48

Blue Hills Of Chicago 53

I'm Like A Cat, You Throw Me Up
In The Air, I'ma Land On My Feet.................... 56

v

You Gotta Cross Your T's
So Muthafuckas Don't Dot Your I's 66

Hood Doctor 73

Jumpin The Border Fence 75

Am I The Devil? 79

Somebody's Gonna Get Killed Today 93

One Last Stop On The Road To Hell 100

Love Birth 106

Time To Upgrade My Package 111

Conclusion 115

EASTSIDE KRAZY

*I used to pack 31 shot glocks in my back
Keep my laces tight
Just in case I need to fight
This drug game didn't change
Just different players
And I'm ten toes deep in it
Relentless in the way I live
Can't sleep because I'm too scared to sit still
Niggas kill
And I'm not getting caught up.
Life's a bitch then you die
So is that the reason so many niggas get high?
I'm just trying to get by
My baby girls need to eat
So I'm out here flipping birds like bacon
Ain't shaking or faking it's eastside krazy
until we all make it*

*Hoping that when it's my time God will understand
And still let me ride by through those pearly gates
Because this is my fate
Or was this my own will
But on the eastside they rob, steal and kill*

Eastside Crazy

Again, I'm just trying to live
Trying to survive
Just playing the cards I was dealt and with each
step I take I try to make It Better
My will to survive
Is strong
Niggas tried and tried but
as a black man I stand strong

I caught bullets all over my body
Shit I even caught a bullet in my lip and nigga
I still won't quit
You cannot silence me
To hell is where I send thee

Desperate times calls 4 desperate measures
And I'm on the bottom of that totem pole
Let them crackers tell it
I refuse to lose
These streets raised me
To be all I could be
I got more done before 6 a.m.
Better than any of them army dudes
These streets are my armed forces and this life
we live is an ongoing war

I just want to live
So my kids can learn and see from me
What not 2 be
I've now learned that it's not just the journey
It's the climb and all that crime
Will only lead to years and years of time.
Don't be like me
Will be the story I tell them
Live by the sword and die by it

Eastside Crazy

Or you can fight 4 life with your mind and refuse
2 commit mental Suicide

No more tears
No more pain
Knowledge of self is my
Eternal gain.
Teaching the youngins that life ain't fair
But the lives you take will never be repaired
A life of crime seems cool until it's your mother
looking with a blank Stare Wondering
where she went wrong
Wondering what she will do
Now that you're dead and gone
Put down those guns and use your mind
As the deadly weapons its supposed 2 be
I am what I am and that I ain't I will never be
I vow this day to shine

Alicia Williams

Eastside Crazy

1

AIN'T KNOW PEACE OVER EAST IN THE BELLY OF THE BEAST

"I always was the underdog, all my life," Melvin Thomas said. He stood on the corner of 95th street kicking an empty bullet shell across the street. Piles of hollow points were scattered everywhere, almost outnumbering the stones on the pavement. When he was a kid, Melvin used to hide behind bushes and throw rocks at cars driving into his hood, but now he shot at them. He grew up around some dudes that were not his friends, and today, it was kill or be killed.

Melvin's heart thumped furiously. He didn't hear the sound of doors locking, windows shutting, or people screaming. Instead, his chest inflated like a balloon as he sucked in breath after breath and limped back to his momma's house a few feet away. His heart was defective (since birth), but adrenaline was surging through his body much faster than blood, and he managed to stay on his feet. If he fell, it would mean death or prison for sure.

Not today though.

His enemies had tried to sneak up on him and blast his ass, but failed to take him out. The only casualty this day would be the moon, which was wrapped in a beard of gun smoke and hung crooked in the sky. Melvin blended into the murky camouflage of night and slipped quietly into his home. Thank God his momma had just left for a midnight shift at the Emerald Park Nursing Home! She gotta earn her $24,000 a year, he thought to himself. Damn, niggas be talking about living in a recession, but I've been living in a recession all my life! His momma busted her ass night after night for a paycheck that he earned in two weeks or by slanging ki's in one day. Just thinking about this made Melvin irritated, but this wasn't the time to start feeling sentimental about his family and their money problems. All that mattered now was getting some rest, because you never knew what was gonna happen tomorrow. Melvin jumped onto his bed, threw on his headphones, and fell asleep listening to Ice Cube.

Today was a good day.

When Melvin Thomas was just 13, a drug empire from "State to the Lake" had been built all around him on the eastside of Chicago. Illegal narcotics were flourishing in an area dripping with poverty and crime, and Melvin was making thousands in a day as a result. The method of operation was not uncommon: claim a corner and get to work. But to do this, you had to have friends, particularly the kind who carry guns and aren't afraid to use them. Kill or be killed, but at the end of the day, it's just "business as usual."

So it was. Melvin joined the infamous Folk gang known as the Black Disciples, or B.D's, around the time he hit puberty. The B.D.'s were founded in 1960 by David Barksdale and became a powerful drug selling institution on Chicago's South and Eastside ghettos for many decades. They also gained international notoriety in 1994 after executing one of their own members, eleven-year-old Robert "Yummy" Sandifer, for killing an innocent bystander during a botched gang shooting on a rival faction, the Gangster Disciples (a.k.a. the G.D.'s). The Black Disciples simply didn't want the bad press or cops breathing down their necks and interfering with their massive drug operation, so Yummy had to die. Of course, Melvin had been well aware of this constant threat on his life even at the hands of his soldiers. Friends were only friends until they didn't pay their dues, show up with the money owed from drugs sold, or flipped to another set or worse, became a snitch. It was the same with other gangs. If you crossed over into their territory or tried to steal their business in some fashion, you became a target. Over 300 B.D. sets have existed annually in Chicago, and with so many people lusting after every dollar to be made from drugs, violence is guaranteed. Wars start, thugs get shot, thugs retaliate, and the deadly cat-and-mouse game, once started, seems to never end.

Yet Melvin had a plan. He didn't want to gang bang or for that matter, really belong even to an organization. His goal was to make money and have fun with his friends and family every minute of his life. Joining the B.D's was not even practical, considering he lived in an all G.D. neighborhood near 95th and Jeffrey. Yet his clique who helped initiate him into the drug business showed him that he couldn't do it alone. Protection under a banner adorned with the Star of

David was necessary. He decided to join the B.D.'s, but in his heart, following others was not really his thing. Armed with a brain for business and soldiers who would protect his enterprise, Melvin would set out to undercut all his competitors in the drug world and eventually claim ownership of a sizeable piece of Chicago's eastside real estate. Bloody battles soon followed, but when it was all over, Melvin was on top. He had become an eastside landlord, living within the Barksdale code of ethics.

2

THE DREAM TEAM

If you asked Melvin whether it was his genetics or his environment that turned him into a hardened gangster, he would definitely choose the latter.

"Everybody always said that Jeffrey Manor was built over a cemetery 'cause there's so much killings. People are scared to come there! I hear people tell me that they never go to the Manor because it's fucking crazy! Yeah, people say it was built over a cemetery, and on it motherfucking hell fell down."

The sky above the Manor was polluted with the ashes of the dead.

The Jeffrey Manor is part of Chicago's South Deering community, one of the seventy-seven official community areas of Chicago. It was once a sprawling neighborhood filled with Jewish families and World War Two veterans who hoped to get a job at the major steel plant in the area, the now defunct Wisconsin Steel Works. When the plant closed its doors around 1980, three thousand workers suddenly were unemployed and without any type of buyout plan. It was a major blow to Chicago's south side, which had at one time been the leader of the American steel industry. Consequently, the neighborhood was inhabited by poverty stricken lower and lower-middle class citizens, sixty per cent of which were black. Nevertheless, the Jeffrey Manor had been soaked in blood long before gangsters were killing each other over drugs and territory. The notorious Richard Speck, who systematically raped and murdered eight student nurses from South Chicago Community Hospital, had committed his atrocious crime at a townhouse located on East 100th street, just a few blocks away from where Melvin grew up on 95th. The killings were a grisly foreshadowing of how violence would saturate the South Deering neighborhood in the years to come. It wasn't too long afterwards, however, that gangs started to claim the Manor as their market place for selling drugs and their warzone to battle for respect and control of turf.

For a brief while, Melvin did not grow up in the Jeffrey Manor. His family had been living in Ada Park, better known as the "Wild Wild 100's." They had moved to eighty-sixth and Ingleside on Chicago's eastside. During the years he lived at these places, both neighborhoods were "doin' the B.D." Melvin developed his networking skills in these communities, being that he was able to go back and visit these places when he became a teenager and began his career as a gangster. Still, the Manor was his stomping grounds.

"Lots of gangstas originated from Jeffrey Manor," Melvin said. "That place was known for gangstas, robberies, and shootings. It was usually three types of people to be seen here, the pimps, the hustlers, and the gangstas. Now a pimp, I respect a pimp, but a pimp always try to bump your bitch behind your back. That's some fuckboy ass shit because if he's your boy, he wouldn't do shit like that to you. A hustler, on the other hand, he will always try to out-hustle you, and get a better price on products that you sell so he can cuff your clientele. That's fuckery right there. But a gangsta, he gonna respect another gangsta. It's a high level of respect with them. The reason is, because if you are a gangsta and DON'T respect another gangsta, it's going to be a problem. And if you're a real man, you going to see eye to eye, 'cause you both know how this can end if it ain't handled properly. Because of this, I always respected gangstas more than anything! And where I live, this applied all the way down the ladder of people. Even the weakest person in the manor was lethal! He would fucking go around in other neighborhoods and make it hard! I mean, the fucking chump of the manor could kill you in a second!

"Like, there was this one cat I'll never forget, he was like a legendary O.G. type who everyone was scared of. They called him Pook G., and hardcore gangstas would hide when he came around, that's how dangerous he was! Pook would roll up, have a gangsta blue pimp Cadillac, tons of money, but at the same time, try to give back to the hood. I remember this high profile dude came to the hood one day, and one of the shortys asked this dude for some money to get ice cream, and he said no. We couldn't believe it! He had all this money and refused to give the kid any. Not even a dollar! Well, that nigga got his ass whipped by Pook and all his money taken. And the best part about it, Pook used that dude's money to buy ice cream for everyone that was there! Man, crazy types of shit like this happened all the time! Pook was the most gangster ass dude coming out of the Jeffrey Manor."

Indeed, gangs had infiltrated every corner of the Jeffery Manor, which was located between 95th street to the north, Torrance Avenue to the east, 103rd Street to the south, and the Chicago & Western Indiana Railroad to the west. The area predominantly belonged to the Gangster Disciples, or G.D.'s. Some of Melvin's friends had chosen the life of a Black Disciple, or B.D., and turned him onto the lifestyle. They knew that being a B.D. in an all G.D. neighborhood meant that stepping outside your door could mean getting shot, but shit happens.

Melvin possessed a bold spirit as well. He would claim the B.D. as his gang affiliation, despite a rivalry between B.D.'s and G.D.'s that escalated just as he was becoming a teen. In the summer of 1991, a series of shootings between the two gangs sparked a division that would become permanent (the G.D.'s used to be called the Black Gangster Disciples and both G.D.'s and B.D.s at one time flew their banners under the notorious David Barksdale).

Still, Melvin hadn't taken it seriously or even wanted to be part of any gang. He was looking mostly for a group to protect him, being that he was born with a septal defect. It made him an easy target for gang members.

"Yeah, they jumped on me, beat me up. When I was a kid, I didn't wanna be no G.D. My big brother was a Mo', so I wanted to be like him at first. Like I said, I was a crybaby that used to get beat up all the time, and when I was about ten years old, I ain't thinking about no motherfucking gangs. I'd go home crying about getting beat up. My brother then made me go out and fight with them.

"Either you going to get your ass whooped by them or you going to get your ass whooped by me!" He said to me.

"Shiiiiit, I didn't want to catch no big brother ass whooping! I went out there and fucked dudes up, and it was what it was. We had all types of gangs in our crew, like the Stones, 4 C.H.'s, G.D's, and B.D.'s., but being the person I was, me and my friends started our own thang. We weren't really a gang at first. It was more of a clique. Everyone that knew who we were made us out to be a gang, I guess because my friends showed me all about the B.D.'s and I took a liking to them or whatever. I mean, B.D.'s was all around me while I grew up in Ada Park and also on Ingleside. But before I knew it, everybody from State to the lake knew about us! I didn't understand it though, because I would see other friends of mine fighting gangs and stuff and thought the shit was a joke.

"Then something happened one day that made me see it differently. One of my partners got kidnapped by the G.D.'s in our neighborhood. Over what I don't know, but they swole him up, and gave him a real nice overnight swelling. Some gangsta shit went on they didn't tell us about, and some of those guys had robbed some dudes in our hood. So it was really more of a power move on the older guys that was in play I guess. As I got older, I learned about that type of gangsta politics. At the time, I was only 13, and I remember some B.D.'s was going to get revenge or something for the kidnapping, and I come downstairs at my B.D. buddy's crib and man, that was the first time I realized that this was some serious shit! This B.D. friend of mine had A.K. 47's, street sweepers, bulldog pumps, glocks, and all types of exotic guns! I thought to myself, damn, everybody down here got a serious face. Like, this ain't no game, this some gangsta shit. The average muthafucka in the hood ain't got these types of guns! This shit is real in the field."

Melvin entered the sixth grade and decided it was time to join a nation of gangstas. He had inked his body with the inscription, "B.D. Melvin." Other tattoos would follow, but this would mark the introduction for him into the Black Disciples. Melvin was no longer alone.

"An older dude I knew brought it to my attention when I was growing up. I was feeling scared, and he said to me "listen, I knew you was going to be special when you was a kid. Now you got a whole gang in front of your name. Your name ain't just Melvin, it's B.D. Melvin. That's a whole gang right there in front of your name."

Melvin not only had the B.D.s behind him, but a group of his closest friends had formed a set under his leadership.

"We're a dream team, known for kicking ass and

taking names, We ended up calling ourselves the Jeffory Manor gangsters, or the JMG Boys. And we diffenitly had manor pride. I had my buddy who was older than all of us but hung out all the time, his name was Big Fred. He was like a super O.G., always guiding us and telling us how to do things. Another one of my buddies was Greedy Greg, A.K.A. Baby Huey, and he was a loyal friend. I had other buddies like Disco who I would fight with, and then there was one of my best buddies in the hood, Little Matty. He was about seven or eight years old when he started hanging out with the O.G.,'s! He got all the respect from everyone, and wasn't anybody younger than this dude. Then I had my main partner in crime Rhonell, who was always there with me. We were tight and did things all the time together. He had my back and I had his.

"I also had a life in the club at a young age, which introduced me to all types of girls. I was meeting girls that were waaay older than me in there! I mean, the first time I fucked a girl, I was nothing but thirteen, maybe fourteen. I think this was when I started to fuck with older girls. It was something about the power I had on the streets that I think made me want to mess with ladies who were mature. That's also why I think I'm more advanced than the average kid. I was fucking ladies who were in their twenties all throughout my teenage years, and at the same time, living in the Jeffrey Manor with the JMG Boys fucking shit up.

"The Manor was my home and always will be. I mean, this cat I knew told me once about cemeteries that the reason they put fences around them is because young niggas are dying to get in, and I think the Manor was like that in a way. Once you were in, you wanted to stay in, and you really couldn't get out except by death or jail. That goddamn neighborhood, it'll do it to you, and it did me good. But I always say to people when I started down this road that I didn't choose this game....THIS GAME CHOSE ME."

3

NOT BOWING TO BOWEN

As a B.D., Melvin had a difficult time going to Bowen High School on East 89th street. The student population is one of the few high schools in Chicago that consistently has an evenly split African-American and Latino background. In the early nineties, Bowen, which is also South Chicago's oldest school, had been known as a place where extreme racial tension, gang activity, and violence manifested on a daily basis. Because of this, Bowen became Chicago's first school to adopt uniforms for every student (circa. 1993), along with parent patrols, security guards, metal detectors, and cameras. Yet Bowen was considered a gang wasteland unsuitable for education by many, including Melvin.

"Drugs were sold everywhere at that place. There was no tile on the floor when you walked in, and no lockers 'cause the lockers were torn out. In one of my classrooms, there was a six point star spray-painted on the chalkboard. I thought to myself how gang signs like this were everywhere on the streets, but in school as well? Damn! The chalkboard was cracked, and looking on the desks, I noticed scribbled on each of them was every fucking gang disrespecting each other. I mean, gangs I ain't ever even heard of, and I'm from the eastside! One year during the first two and half weeks of school, there was a shooting every day. Folks and Mo's was shooting at each other daily. I'm saying to myself, Momma, what the fuck I'm being sent to, Eastside High? You tell me to go to school, and I'm going to get killed!

"One time my momma came to see my teachers in school, she saw it for herself. One of my guys came up to me and told me it was going down with some dudes. "Melvin let's go beat these dude's asses," he said to me.

"Don't you see my momma standing right there?" I replied.

"My momma just looked at me and shook her head. I mean, what was I supposed to do? I couldn't go fight with her there! So my momma talked to one of my teachers, and my teacher told her bluntly, "Fights like this happen all the time."

"Like this shit is normal, all the fighting. Of course, my momma was surprised, but I wasn't. The teachers weren't teaching us anything anyways. Looking back, I realize it was good though that I had a lot of fights in school, 'cause it made me real good at fighting. I had to fight just to keep going to school. I had to be wild. I remember an incident where I had to knock this muthafucka out who was constantly messing with me. I was scared of him, but when he walked right up to me in school one day talking shit to me, I just knocked his ass out with one punch. He could have whooped me too. That's when I was really starting to get my juice though.

"The only problem was that things were too fucked up at Bowen. There were so many different types of gangs other than the one I belonged to that went there. All us Folks were outnumbered at Bowen. I mean, my wrestling coach was a Latin King Gang member! If him and his guys caught me outside or something, ain't no teachers gonna stop them from hurting me. I told my momma how scared I was of the wrestling coach, but it didn't matter to her. All she cared about was that I went to school. So when I had knocked that one dude straight out, the wrestling coach and some of the Mo's chased the shit out of me! I knew it was going to be me or them, but I got away. So at Bowen, I learned there that I could fight well, and nine times out of ten, if I hit somebody, I would knock them out.

"I think I was also distracted because I was popular in school back then, despite not ever attending. I always liked the girls, and I always have been a silly dude, telling jokes and pulling pranks. That is, when I wasn't fighting. I was always like that to every girl I met. You know, if a cute girl starts smiling, you got her. I would be eyeballing all the girls I liked and at the same time, I was a leader type. I have never been a follower, so I would make sure I could hold my own. I was always going back and forth between flirting with girls and getting into fights. I guess that's why I ended up getting kicked out of school there for fighting. Every school I went to though, it was the same. I would fight and sometimes win, but sometimes get my ass whooped too. It wasn't all glory."

Besides, how can a student be out on the streets

selling drugs all night and then try to wake up at seven o' clock in the morning for school? Melvin said goodbye to the classroom and attended school on the streets, where he would graduate with a degree in selling drugs and getting paid.

"I wanted to get plenty money," Melvin said.

A typical family living in the Jeffery Manor consistently made a combined household income of just $34,000 a year. His mom made even less than that. Yet Melvin noticed certain people around him were living in luxury. He also saw how others reacted when these people would demonstrate their wealth on the streets. "I was with this girl walking to the bus stop. I was about ten, and we walked by a dope boy riding past in his car. He had an expensive ride, big rims, loud stereo, and everything else. I saw how she looked at him with these big wide eyes, so I said to myself, man, I got to have that! I GOT TO HAVE THAT!"

"That's when shit started going down."

4

PURSE FIRST AND ASS LAST

Melvin was introduced to selling weed when he was twelve, which was nothing unusual in the Jeffrey Manor. His best friend, Rhonell, had been selling dope since he was nine years old. Melvin considered him more advanced than he was when it came to drugs.

"Everybody knew I was doing some lightweight shit selling weed, but anytime I sold it to somebody, they were also smoking rocks. And these addicts always be asking me for some damn rocks when I sold to them! I started thinking about why I wasn't getting the best of both worlds by selling both of them together. So, I started selling crack. I sold my first bag, but I didn't take it seriously. The dude I was getting my drugs from used to be mad at me 'cause I got so fucking good at it and then acted like I didn't care! I got all my money in the safe, and when I open up the safe and let that dude count it, I would leave him alone with the money.

"I'm gonna go outside and play," I would tell him.
"He would yell at me, say, "Man, what's your problem?! I could beat the shit out of you right now and take this!"

"I would just laugh and tell him "I trust you, now I'm going outside to play."

"I still ain't take it serious though. I just sold a couple of bags to get a nice outfit or a new rap tape to listen to. I think people at school knew what was up 'cause I was still going at the time, but I was always doing stuff in school to get in trouble. Like I would get suspended from school, and I'd come back with an Adidas outfit or a Puma outfit on. There I was, with a brand new outfit, just coming off suspension. I used my time away from school to make money and buy clothes! My one friend Disco, picked a fight with me over this shit."

"You get suspended for three days and you come back with a new outfit on, I don't like it," he said.
"And then we got into a fight. He got the first punch in and then it was on. I think, overall, we had like three fights about it. In the end, it worked out though because he was the one that taught me to steal on muthafuckas before they steal on me. He always stole on me first."

Melvin gradually moved into a more serious drug operation, but back then, it was really just about having the pimpest outfit.

"Yeah, Rhonell, he jumped off the porch earlier than me. By the time he was eleven, he was gangbanging too. And we would hang out all the time, he had money and I really didn't have that kind of money he had. He used to buy me daily doubles at McDonalds so you know this was a long time ago.

"One day, he said, "man, I ain't about to keep buying you daily doubles, you have to start selling your own shit." And he had looked out for me, put money in my pocket. He bought me an outfit here, a pair of shoes there, but I really wasn't into it. That's when he gave me my first eight-ball, and I ain't looked back since.

"Selling was easy for us too. Back then, we were always running up to hypes. Down the street, over here, over there. We were constantly trying to beat each other to the cars. All the while, I got a fresh ass outfit on and he got a fresh outfit on too.

"Aw, man," he would challenge me. "Wait 'til tomorrow." And we would each sell a fifty pack or something for the day. That's five hundred dollars, and that was cool for a day's work. Then we would laugh and say, "tomorrow I'm going shopping." It went on like this until I had the freshest outfit on the block. And that's how me and my partner did it.

"I really came up after Rhonell was sent to a group home, then juvenile detention, and finally prison. There were a couple of other guys that I fucked with on the block, but they disappeared too. One of my partners went to jail for murder at age twelve. Another buddy on the block got forty years for murder and armed robbery. One more after that got thirty three years for the same thing. Everybody got locked up on me, so basically I started to be out there by myself a lot of times. I had the whole block to myself.

"It wasn't easy though. The dream team was just

starting to come together, and I was still surrounded by dudes I couldn't trust. A lot of people were trying to hurt me, but I outdid them. Nobody had really wanted to give me or my friends wings and let us fly, but by the end, we were at the top of the game in the Jeffrey Manor.

"Some people I could trust, like my friend Big Homie. Every city got a guy like Big Homie. He was a grimy ass nigga that was into all types of shit like selling drugs and robbery, anything he could find to keep his pockets filled. He was a real authority on selling. This guy was also a super cool dude and a playa type. He was really laid back, and truthfully was the opposite of us. He first took me under his wing and then gave me my wings and let me fly. He never really cared about red or blue banners, or any gang stuff at all for that matter. He only wanted to know if he could make money with you. That's all he cared about. So I would always say to him, "purse first and ass last. Let's get this money!"

5

YOU GOTTA CHARGE IT TO THE GAME

Melvin was on his way to becoming the dope dealer he saw driving down the street. He bought his first of many cars.

"Man, at fifteen, I had a car and I mean, my momma ain't never had a car. I liked that I got things she couldn't afford to buy. And the fucked-up part about it, the way she found out about me having a car is one day my buddy saw my car tire was flat and told my momma to let me know. She looked at him funny and said that I didn't own a car. But I did, and she got upset. I think that's when she really became aware of what I was doing. But it didn't stop me from driving a brand new Chevy with hammers, candy apple regals, and the deep dish 30's and vogues. That was the shit back then."

Melvin's drug business grew to the point where it was becoming a full-time affair. At sixteen, he started selling ki's. "I was on like a half a ki and I was getting plenty of money. But it used to take more time cooking the drugs than selling it. My momma used to always trip on me. I had lines around the block man waiting for my product. I would have to sometimes even cook up a ki or two at once, but when I cook them up, they were already gone. The drugs got so bad with all the people coming up to the house, and my ma, she knew I was selling drugs. She didn't approve of it, but what could she do? I was growing up with no father. I mean, he wasn't around all the time, and here I was able to help her out with the money I was making. She didn't like what I was doing, but she was struggling so she ain't say nothing. I kept going and going with selling until I was on top and she dealt with it in her own way."

Besides the lack of parental control, one of the major reasons for Melvin's skyrocket style ascension was his ability to undercut all competition with a genius marketing tactic.

"I was noticing, everyone in the neighborhood was selling their ounces for eight hundred or whatever. So I sold mine for five hundred. I was selling ounces like dime bags! It got to the point where other drug dealers want to buy off me so they could sell their shit in other hoods! I was selling ten ounces for the price of nine ounces. Soon it wasn't just the block I had, I got the whole neighborhood to sell to and it was hard to keep up with it all! "

A frenzy began over Melvin's cheap prices, which brought out all kinds of interesting types to his doorstep.

"Crack heads bringing all types of shit to my door, you'd be surprised! My connect had the same thing happen to him too. A lot of crack heads showed up with guns of all kinds, electronics, chain saws, whatever they could get their hands on for trade.

You hear them be saying to me "Yeah, I got a glock nine, let me get an eight ball." Damn! This crack head want an eight ball for it? It's a five-six hundred dollar gun! I gave his ass a half eight ball, just like a little eight.

"One of the things I got the most was cars. I probably had about forty cars in my life, if not more. I had so many cars, man! It wasn't even funny. Pretty cars and hoopties, and man, I loved hoopties. You get more money in a hooptie, and nobody really pay any attention to you when your in that car. But anyways, it was crazy how these crack heads became like animals."

Consequently, Melvin had to work extra hard to keep up with the constant flow of customers looking to score a fix. "My momma told me, "I knew you was going to be a muthafucka, 'cause I went blind with your ass!" But I never knew I would be this much of a threat or this much of a dope dealer! My buddy Disco, he even told me, "the way you hustle is scary." I said to him, "damn, scary?" He just looked at me and said, "I never seen no shit like that in my life." I had like, at one point, four ki's all gone in such a fast time and he couldn't believe how fast I was getting rid of the product. I was good at it. Hell yeah, I even put in overtime. What the fuck they say? **I just love my job!**"

As the nineties progressed, so did Chicago's war on drugs. An aggressive campaign by law enforcement had caused many drug operations to expand into other cities. Melvin's operation was not particularly affected, but the idea to expand into other American cities rooted in his mind as a result of the Chicago police force's efforts to push drugs out of communities.

"I was delirious. I was going everywhere. I mean, I was doing my thang in Chicago but I like to go out and travel a lot, like to the small towns where dimes go for fifties. Then I decided because I like travelling and because everywhere people were being pushed out by the law or other hood factions, I went to other places I never thought about going before. Like Milwaukee, Iowa, or wherever. Even small towns like Springfield. It was all the small towns that made sense to me. Guys go to the small towns to triple their profit. Lots of people didn't know when to quit though. I mean, I knew how to read people. I could go to the towns, fuck with four or five people.... that's more smarter and safer than anything else I was doing up in Chicago. And I was never greedy, man. When I go into Chicago, everybody is greedy there, and that's what messed so many people up. We hustle for our neighborhood, and everybody had their own area and own way of getting money. The problem is that gangstas are so greedy, they get to robbing and fighting and gangbanging over everything they want for themselves."

Despite being aware of the dangers in robbing, Melvin was not impervious to it.

"One of my partners, his name was 2 Big, he was part of the dream team, and was one gangsta ass dude. He was robbing everybody, man. I called him my "jeweler." He used to give me a lot of jewelry, like Rolexes, diamond earrings, chains with diamonds in them, ten karat bracelets, you name it. He used

Eastside Crazy

to sell me jewelry for the lo' lo'. He was robbing entertainers, rappers, and big time dope boys. This nigga had a disease, man. It was called robbing. He was terrorizing the city, robbing muthafuckas day and night. Everybody knew to watch out for him.

"2 Big had my back though. Like, one time, I robbed these four different dudes all at the same time. I took their money and told them, "I'll be back." Well, I got like fifty-some thousand from those idiots. But the bad part about it, somebody right after that ended up stealing like $17,000 from me!

"How the fuck the robber got robbed?" I yelled at 2 Big. I was so upset at what happened to me. "That defeats the fucking purpose!" You know what 2 Big told me?

"You gotta charge it to the game."

"I said to him, "What you mean? You take shit all day!" I replied, but he just laughed.

"You are the smartest dummy I know," he said.

"I eventually slowed up on the robbing because you catch too much bad luck behind it. I mean, the only real crazy robbing I ever did was one time, I snatched some dude out of a club. This was the nineties man, we were young and hungry and we knew we could maybe get a lot of money doing this type of stuff. I snatched his ass and made everyone around him nervous. He had a gun too, and it was the biggest motherfucking gun I ever seen in my life! So my man pulled up in my car and we told this dude to get his ass in the car. He saw us and immediately knew we weren't playing. His was wearing a nice Rolex and diamond studded earrings, but at that time, I said to myself, damn! I hope my partners ain't lying to me! I was told he was worth five hundred thousand! He might not be worth that much. This made me angry, so as he was getting in the car, I smacked him with my pistol and he went down with his ass in the air. He had his gun, but I had the ups on him, so I made him get in and put the power seat as close to the dash as possible. His whole body was smooshed against the dash, so he couldn't get to his gun. I jumped in the back seat and my partner drove off.

"Damn, what we going to do man? Let him go?" My partner said to me. He was nervous and sweaty.

"Hell nah! I want some money out of this shit!" I answered.

Night flung a blanket of darkness over them for protection. It was time to get paid.

"We ended up getting twenty thousand out of him, a bezzled out watch, and his earrings. But the crazy part about it, we drove off to some secluded spot and took his phone out and called the last number on the callback. Our plan was going to tell one of his guys that we were holding the dude for ransom. So we called the number and a guy answered the phone. "Look, we want five hundred thousand or we going to kill his bitch ass," I said.

"Five hundred thousand?' The guy answered in shock. "GOOOOOD LOOOORRDD!"

"I couldn't believe he said that! We was laughing so hard in the background that we had to hang up and call back. The way he said it was so funny. Even the dude we kidnapped was laughing. We call the guy back and say, "O.K., we want a hundred and twenty-five thousand." The guy gasped. "Hundred and twenty-five thousand? GOOOOD LOOOORRDD!"
"Oh man...we just hung up and laughed. I didn't even want to talk to this dude. I just took what the guy had on him. Fuck it. What could we do?"

6

THE BLACK STEVE-O

Even though Melvin had occasionally participated in robberies, his everyday life while growing up as young pup consisted of drug selling, drinking, and getting high.

"My Uncle Pete gave me my first joint when I was about six. He was driving his Regal with gangsta white walls and I was sitting on his lap pretending to be driving. I couldn't reach the pedals, and he enjoyed letting me be the one in charge. I started to smell something funny behind me, and when I looked at him, he had a joint hanging out from between his lips. I was curious about it. He saw the expression on my face, and that's when he told me, "hit this."

"I hit the joint and then blew the smoke out like I seen people do. I didn't know what I was doing though.

"Nah, hit it and suck it in," he said to me. He laughed and patted me on my head. So I sucked it in and started coughing like crazy!!! I never forget what he said after this:

"This is what I DON'T want you to do."

"I was like, "well, why the fuck you give it to me then?"

"Because the first time you did it, I wanted it to be with me," he answered.

"Whatever though. I slept for like two days after that. My mother didn't understand what was going on. She would have whooped my motherfucking ass if she knew I was smoking and doing drugs."

However, Melvin wasn't the only one doing drugs in his family. His older brother headed down a path towards drugs even before he did. Likewise, Melvin's father was also involved in narcotics. The only person in his life who actually didn't do drugs was his mother.

"Drug problems ran through my family like Katrina ran through New Orleans. At an early age, my dad started having drug problems, smoking weed and crack," Melvin said. "He was still on my ass though. He wouldn't let me do shit. But I ain't got no bad thing to say about him. It was just that in the eighties, crack destroyed a lot of families. My dad continued to battle with crack cocaine throughout my life, and my parents were on and off ever since I was a kid. They only recently got divorced. I mean, once you get going on the drugs, you start to slip away a little. You get too busy. It was the same with my brother. We never hung out much. He was also too busy doing his own thing. I mean, he graduated and lived his life and all that, but he's fighting a drug problem now, and still dealing with a lot of them drugs. Smoking them damn primos. Maaan, that's some stinky shit! He's still my nigga even if he gets no bigger!"

I lost myself in gray clouds. Down the spiral of a pipe and a plant, stepping in and out of reality. I wondered how much longer I could go this way before I became the painting on the wall and not the person looking at it.

"Somebody asked me what was the most playa ass shit I ever did, and I think maybe it was this one time, me and two of my guys had a little bit of our product with us and we was at one of my cribs. I definitely tried to have two or three cribs at once to hang at. So I ain't got no raw, but I had cut open a ki and started passing it around. And man, we was higher than giraffe pussy! I cut it open and we tooted it right out of the ki. I never got a plate or nothing. I left them with the ki in my crib and I told them to do as much as they wanted to. Use it, don't abuse it. Enjoy yourself. I was making above the extra. There was so many grams to go around. And I know they're going to take some with them too. Muthafuckas be cutting a hole in the ki, tooting it. It was some real certified playa, gangsta shit.

"We used to toot raw for like two days, man, be high as a motherfucker! After you get so high for two days, you feel like a fucking loser. You can't really get high no more, and you want to just go into a closet and hide. I could be a walking time bomb, speed balling like I was. For instance, I shot my friend. We were hanging out, and I was already so fucking high. We started talking shit to each other, just joking around, but then he made a quick move around me. He reached for my gun and tried to take it, but there wasn't no playing around with that. So I shot him, but I was so high, I really didn't know what I did! I shot him in the leg. Thankfully, he wasn't hurt that bad.

"It got like that with all the drugs I was using. I also saw a lot of other niggas doing so many drugs that they turned crazy!! I knew that shit would fuck you up, but that's how it was. I was telling people around me, "this shit is to be sold, not told.

"In my neighborhood, it was like a fucking tradition to toot raw. I mean, I used to get so high, you'd think I was the black Steve-O. Tootin' raw, poppin pills, four or five at a time. I ain't never tried heroin or anything. I mean, I wouldn't even challenge myself 'cause it ain't nothin good for my body. I just stuck with the pills, weed, and raw.

"I smoked a sherm stick (a joint dipped in P.C.P.) on accident before. One of my homies from the hood, he would get wet. You know, cush and all that type of reefer would come into play with this cat, so I thought maybe that's what he was into.

"Let me hit that motherfucking weed," I said to him. I was hitting it hard too. My man was like, "you hitting that shit so hard, that's not regular weed."

"So what? I smoke dro before, it's nothing."

"That shit ain't dro," he retorted. I still was hitting it."

"He spoke up."

"It's perm."

"Perm?" I asked. "What's perm?"

"It's sherm, nigga!!" And he started laughing like crazy. As soon as he said that, it kicked in. Damn! I was fucked up to the fifth power!"

The drugs and partying was fun for Melvin for awhile, but later in life, it would become tiresome and repetitive for him.

"I'm the type of dude, I get tired of something quick. I used to smoke cigarettes but one day, I just stopped cold turkey. I used to toot raw all the time as well. I started smoking weed when I was a teenager. Now, not at all. I mean, I don't think I can get addicted to nothing."

7

EVERY LESSON IS STILL A BLESSING

Melvin's carefree antics of robbing, drinking, and partying had caught the attention of police and other law enforcement officials. It seemed his days outside of a jail cell were numbered.

"First time I dropped out of school, I had gone to Cook County Jail that same week. What happened was that I was hanging with this real, grimy ass, loser gangsta. He had murdered and committed all types of heinous crimes, and the judge even had called him a "menace to society." I'm like, daaaamn, I thought that was just a movie! This guy had got locked up so many times. His list of priors included things like murder in '85, murder in '89, murder in '91, double murder in '93. My momma started crying to people, saying "who's my baby with?" I eventually had to cut him off, but before I did, we robbed muthafuckas left and right. I just got caught up. We would take their guns, money, whatever they had on them, we would sneak up and take it all. It was a treat more than a robbery!

"Then one day, we was breaking into some dude's house and got busted for a home invasion. So I had to try and pay this muthafucka I was robbing five thousand, 'cause he was going to court and if he said anything, I'd be fucked. I was going to pay him five thousand to change his statement. Well, I sat in jail for three weeks 'cause I only had a thousand put up, and my bond was two thousand. I said to myself, Shiiiit, I ain't never going thru this again. I gotta make bail.

"Thankfully, Big Homie knew a lawyer who understood what we were up to out in the world. The lawyer would tell us, "Man, you guys are all like gangstas!" He made us laugh, but he was smart and knew how to handle our cases and make them look different than what they really were about. He kept it one hundred with me. So I got out, paid that muthafucka off I had tried to rob, and if it wasn't for me, that dude would still probably be in jail for that. I got us help with this lawyer and he got us off that charge. They were trying to give me thirty to sixty years and this was my first case! I dodged a bullet, but how was I supposed to know I could face a thirty to sixty year sentence for the shit I'd done? It wasn't the last time though for me.

"I mean, my dumb ass, I took a pistol case for one of my dudes. Loyalty was my thing. I was a loyal dude, man. But I was loyal to the wrong people. Like they say, you gotta keep your grass cut low so you can see the snakes. Dudes come as friends but they are really foes. I think that's why I always wouldn't let nobody get in my circle. Didn't matter who they were or if they were pros at their business. I had been fucked so much out of money by a lot of people. Unfortunately, with this case about this muthafucka with the pistol, we were driving someplace and cops stopped us. He had a gun on him and he told me he's on probation. The police found the pistols on the passenger side of the car. So I took the pistol case. I didn't really have a background, and the police said to me, "Melvin, we're putting it on dude, and whoever takes it, we don't care, but if nobody takes it, we're putting it on him." I was going to the county anyway for a warrant at this time, but I thought this muthafucka was my friend. He really wasn't.

"Then I got caught on another pistol case when I was out riding around with Rhonell and with two guns in my Cadillac truck. I mean, every day I left my home, I was committing a felony with my gun being always on me. What could I do? I had to have protection. The thing is, somebody had to have told on me. I had my gun hid in a custom stash spot inside the Cadillac and the cops, when they pulled me over, they popped the stash spot right open. There I was, me and Rhonell, my best friend, driving around, and I had just bought me and him leather outfits. We were treating ourselves. And now we both got busted for the guns. I got one put on me, and Rhonell got the other one put on him.

"That's the thing I wanna say, when I was doing wrong, I didn't have my credentials right. A lot of things could have been prevented. Like, I'm driving a fifty-some thousand dollar car but don't have a license. The cops stop me and find out I ain't got no license, they instantly cuffed me up. I was on probation for nine months.

"On the gun charge with Rhonell, the motherfucking states attorney tried to make out the case to be way worse than I think it really was, talking about my gun being a nine millimeter and I had it loaded because I wasn't going out like Relly Rell. I couldn't believe she knew who that was! I mean, Relly was a guy from our community that got killed in some gangster shit. The states attorney asked me if I knew him and when my lawyer tried to object, the judge overruled him and told me he wanted to hear what I had to say. So the second I mentioned I knew him from around the neighborhood, the jury convicted me. That's all they needed to hear.

"When I went to the joint this time for the guns, I knew it might be for a long time. What was I supposed to do though? I started to get nervous, but luckily, my lawyer had worked out a deal with the prosecution. "He told me, "look you got a choice: go to the joint for two months or do two years probation."

"I mean, two years probation that included seven P.M. curfews, urine drops, and random visits from a probation officer? No fucking way. So my lawyer recommended I do the two months and be done with the charge. At this time, I had never been to the joint. I'ma young adult and could still make moves on the street even from behind bars, so I thought why not? I could see what the joint looked like.

"I did the time, but it was the longest two months of my life. Sixty-one days and I never want to do it again."

What's that smell? Is it the dirty bars that keep me from running the streets? Maybe it's the stench that rises in the air from hundreds of toilets in all the cells that are filled with shit. Prisoners reek of sweat, cheap soap, and lies.

Maybe that smell that won't leave me alone is the smell of sulfur. This is another level of hell….

Prison was not a place that Melvin really wanted to see again. He was incarcerated at Illinois River Correctional Center in Canton, Illinois. His sentence was for a year but he ended up doing sixty-one days. Illinois River is a level three high security prison that holds, on any single day throughout the year, at least 1,950 adult males, many of them violent offenders.

"I went to Illinois River, but first I went to Joliet, did a physical there, then on to Stateville for about a week and a half. Then to Illinois River. I mean, Stateville was everything people say it was. It was the worst one I been to, but Illinois River wasn't any fun either. I didn't get a shower when I was in Stateville and barely had a chance in Illinois River to stay clean. They don't feed you enough either. Every time I worked out in there, I was hurting. They feed you enough food to get the knot up out of your stomach and that's it, man. I also met a couple of smooth brothers there but I ain't really took a liking to any of them. I never wanted new friends.

"That's how my buddy Suga Free got killed. This one nigga had got out of the joint, and the first thing he did was shoot Suga Free in the back of the head, then shoot him eighteen more times while he was lying on the ground. And the dude who shot him was his cell mate in jail. Suga Free didn't even really know him. I always thought about that every minute when I was in prison. Even my pops told me not to trust a convicted felon, because they will do anything not to go back. Just understand them and stay away from their asses.

"I think about Suga Free and what happened, and I remember that he gave me ten thousand when I came out of the joint for those two months. He did it so pimpalicious too."

"This is for all the times I fucked up your money, man, or you got me out of jail," He said to me with his hands outstretched."

"It made me appreciate him. Suga Free was the type of dude who could get a lick for two hundred thousand easy, and he knows if he tells me, I want in. We were hip mates for a long time. He lifted from that guy and then it was over. Rest in peace, Suga Free.

"You know too, I think about the fact that people like Suga Free got killed and spent all that time in jail, and I took it for what it was worth. Every lesson was still a blessing."

Time

That's what they call it because that's all you got
I was riding high on the wings of life
before I got locked!
Sure there was struggle and strife
But my struggle was my hustle
And I didn't punch nobody's clock!
I made rocks pop!
The world was my oyster
And I found pearls on every corner

Pound after pound
More shots
More rounds
I got high so I could fly
Through those battle grounds!
Those bullets were flying
Burning right through me
But I couldn't feel it
My adrenaline was fueling!
Hittin' those streets early in the morning
At night I lay in the bed feeling
Cold and lonely
My story is an old one
But my end doesn't have to be
Each time those bars locked behind me
I knew it'd be for life
But God didn't see fit to let that be
And I still don't know why
Instead of doing better
I reached for a bigger slice of the pie
I'm sure many nights
I made God cry

Eastside Crazy

I know because I felt it
All those dark skies
But what was I supposed to do?
I didn't even know who I had become!
What had I really truly done to end up
A fallen son?

My life seemed like it had been waste of time
Days and days without sunshine
I could see it in the eyes
Of that crack fiend's son
Did he see me when I sold
His father those drugs?
Did he hate me for being the one
Who had helped his father be
What he had become?
I couldn't trip!

His father's hit would add to more money
That would fill up more zips
I wasn't
Thinking about how that rock
Could start or stop a clock
That rock could have been the beginning and end
For that kid
In so many ways
I introduced him to the game
The fucked up game
Of a street nigga's life!

I had to keep moving
But how could I continue pursuing this life?
Drugs!
Guns!

Eastside Crazy

*The only way to play this game
was without feeling
No remorse
So to ease my mind
I started doing lines
Just to get by
Or maybe to justify the lives I was tainting
And my life that was wasting
Every step I took
Was not without medication.
To numb the pain and enjoy my street fame?
To earn respect
From this sadistic game?
Shit, I guess everybody did know my name!
My name had power!
The kind that sent fear
That rushed down like a razor shower!*

*I got kids to feed was my reason
I got to take care of me
Because no one else will
My mama threw me out
But who could blame her?
How you gonna sell dope
To yo' mamma's neighbors?*

*The jail time wasn't easy
But then it was never long either
And each time I got out
I'd sing that same ol' song
Money, Power, Respect!
But then cocaine
Became my closest friend
Swallowed with pills
And bottles of gin!*

Eastside Crazy

Sin was more than a notion
As I soared high on this roller coaster
The one I created
Not the one God fated

I looked in the mirror
And hated the reflection
Wondering how I messed up
God's perfection
My reflection stared at me
With malice in his eyes
And even though I'd smile
It was only a disguise
Behind it there was my shame trying hard
To cover my pain
I felt like I was trapped inside
Of an insane game
No winners
Only losers
Lucifer was throwing the dice
And doing the choosing!
Every day was a gamble

And every time I'd dodge a bullet
My mind would scramble

They trying to kill me while I'm still in!
What's gon' happen if I get out?
When does it stop?
How can it end?
Will I ever be able to trust again?
I don't want to play anymore now that I know
I can't win
It took me a long time but finally

Eastside Crazy

I gave in
I learned my lesson
Each day is a blessing!
It's another chance to change the world
Instead of continuing to infest it!

Alicia Williams

8

CLUBS, CARS, AND BIG RAP STARS

Melvin and his homies were called eastside landlords. They took care of the people around them and fought off competition in the drug trade down in Chicago's south side ghetto. Along with this, Melvin and the Jeffrey Manor Gangster Boys made all the streets from "State to the lake" their personal stomping grounds. They went to work all day and night, but they also enjoyed life as gangstas who had a solid monopoly of selling crack and dope to even the poorest junkie. Their low prices kept everyone coming back and consequently, kept their pockets full. Melvin liked being in control, and except for the cops who fucked with him every once in awhile and opposing gang sets trying to claim territory, or huge gangs like G.D.'s always looming in the background, he found a way to survive in style.

"I never expected to see 21, man. I ain't give a fuck about anything, I was living so crazy. I was popping pills, running my drug game all through my teenage years, and drinking so much Tanqueray I coulda been a spokesperson for them. I had the whole hood drinking Tanqueray! That shit is like liquid crack. But man, I always expected the worst on everything, so I wouldn't be so disappointed if it didn't go right.

Eastside Crazy

Then 21 came and I was like, damn, I'm still here!

"I realized that in my life, I had collected so many things and done a lot. I had people out there for me who were like money machines. I was getting capital all the time, and because of this, I had a lot of things. I liked to buy shoes, so I got a hundred-some pair of them! I had a lot of apartments too. I always kept two or three cars at the same time. I had a fancy car, a hustle car, and an everyday car. One of my cars was a Lumina, back when they first got big. It was real pimpish. I put these rims on the car that were called wishbones. They were the rims with all the fancy decorations on them. I pushed amps in the back that got the loud music blasting with no problems inside it. The guy who put my system in the car got killed, but I used him for a lot of my cars. And I rolled with style.

"I had a lot of other nice things with my cars too. I mean, I had custom stash spots in many of my cars. When you hit the A.C. and press the rear defroster buttons, the whole dash come up. But that's why I went to prison, the cops knew about that one. Still, something spiffy always catches my motherfucking eye. Me and a couple of my partners, we were always good at dressing up cars. Dudes would even come get me to help them dress up their cars. People looked at their stuff differently after I helped them. I was always sharing with my partners like that! My motto was simple:

"**It's a treat when players meet!**"

"I had money and I think everyone started to know

it. I mean, even the clothing stores, they knew I had money, and they would call me up and tell me they got some new stuff so I could come check it out before anyone else. I would throw on my new clothes and look pimpalicious everywhere I go!

"So, anyways, when I was dressed up and looking nice, me and my partners would hit up all the clubs. Our favorite spot was called "The Other Place." It was on 75th and King Drive. We had so many fights in that club I don't know why they kept letting us in there. We would always take a girl home, or just bust them down outside in the car. We fucked that spot up for sure. I think we were the reason they ended up closing down. But it was our spot, and we had a couple more spots just like it. So we were at clubs all night hanging out, keeping tight, and listening to the most gangsta music that was hot at the time. Some of these rappers were like me in a lot of ways."

Indeed, rappers like the New Orleans based Hot Boyz (who, at one time, featured Juvenile, Lil Wayne, and several other members who were part of Cash Money Records), 2 Pac, Notorious B.I.G., and Ghetto Boys rapper Scarface all reflected Melvin's life.

"I listened to a lot of rappers, from Pac to B.I.G. and of course, my man, Scarface. He probably wouldn't even remember me, but one time on a Memorial Day weekend in Miami, I heard somebody scream, "hey Face!" I turned around just when he turned around, and we saw each other, and I started talking to him. The only thing I said to him was, "I been in this game thirteen years and I ain't went nowhere." It was a lyric from one of his songs. Before I knew it, he said to everyone about me, "Damn, I like this little nigga right here. "I was so happy he said that, me and my homies ended up taking all kinds of pictures with him and we were flashing gang signs in the pictures. Face was real cool and down to earth.

"Another group that was always part of what I was into was them Hot Boyz. Me and my partners went Hot Boyz crazy! They remind me of when I was on stage at a big rap concert with all kinds of different rap stars, and while they were rapping, all of the people were putting their hands at their feet. Out of nowhere, these hot girls were being grabbed and put up on the stage. I started playing with their pussies, and then another girl got brought up onstage and started licking this one bitch's pussy. The crowd went wild. The security was yelling at me onstage, saying that there were kids out in the crowd, but we were just having fun, and now that I really think about it, I was so drunk that I didn't care at all. I had wanted to just do some spontaneous shit!"

9

THESE GIRLS ARE B.D. ANGELS

For Melvin, a huge part of his life outside of gangbanging and drugs was the crazy times with women.

"I always had a gang of bitches, man. I was quick on my toes when it came to them hoes. I had ugly girls, hustlin' girls. I mean, women always took a liking to me, man. There are a lot of girls with my name tattooed on their ass. Lots of them, man. I stopped counting after about fifteen or twenty. At least thirty girls got my name stamped on them. Used to be my thing: Brand the ho!

"I got into all kinds of crazy sex stuff with girls. I was always fascinated by two girls kissing. I was infatuated with that for years. One time, I had these two girls with me and we were popping some x pills, and that turned out to be the best threesome I ever had. One of them was chocolate and thick, the other one was chocolate mixed with caramel, and had big-ass sexy titties! I had both of them girls with me, and both of them liked me, man. One of them said she had a threesome before, so the other one said that's what she wanted to do. It was her fantasy to have a threesome with another girl.

"So I got both of them together, picked them up, and took them downtown to Benihanas. I'ma playa, man, and I do big boy restaurants, 'cause that's how I was taught. In the rap songs, they say, "gangstas and pimps eats lobsters, and shrimps." That's what the Hot Boyz said, and that's how we played it.

"So anyways, I had these two girls, and they order their drinks and everything, and everybody got to loosening up. Me and the two girls and these two other couples were sitting at the table, and we were eating enough to be good for the night. Pretty soon, the x pills kicked in, and I was breezy as fuck. When we were finishing up, I looked over and saw that these two girls were kissing at the table.

"Oh! Damn!" I said, and these dudes at the table with their girls, they laughed. "That's what I'm talking about," I said.

But a girl at another table elbowed her guy and stared at them.

"What the fuck is wrong with these bitches?" I heard her say.

They about to start some shit up in this muthafucka. "Can we get this to go? Excuse me, can we wrap that up?" I said. This other girl who was sitting with her boyfriend at another table, she hollered to one of my girls, "that's what I'm talking about!"

"Aw shit!" I said while laughing.

Her guy was like, "bitch, what? What the fuck?"

Eastside Crazy

I tried to get us out of there fast.

"Can you please hurry up with that?" I said. I pointed to both my girls and said, "you two muthafuckas, y'all need Jesus!"

We left and got the fuck out of there before trouble started.

"When we left, I had got a room and we went there immediately. And everything was just on point. I had got a jacuzzi room, so we were all in the jacuzzi. Man, before you know it, they jumped out. So I'm chilling in the jacuzzi by myself, and they were getting down on each other, and I'm watching them. Then they got to sucking on each other.

"Damn, my dick is harder than Chinese arithmetic and I heard Chinese arithmetic is pretty hard!" I said. "So after a while, they were getting down for about ten, fifteen minutes, and I'm chilling, trying to be a player about the situation. I finally just gotta touch them. Both of those girls got to serving me as soon as I did! One is sucking my dick, and one is licking my balls, and I was breezy as fuck and seeing in 3D! After they finished sucking on me, the one girl hopped on the bed and immediately spread her legs for me to fuck her. I started long dicking her slowly, and the other girl sat on her face. She was facing me, so I leaned forward and kissed her neck, and she reciprocated by licking me from my ear down to my chest. I ain't even gonna lie, I ate some pussy that night too. OOH boy!

"Damn! This shit is like the movies!" I said.

Eastside Crazy

"I definitely should have had some footage on that. But it was a beautiful thing, man, and the crazy part about it was coming out of the hotel the next day, I met this dude who was like, "playboy, I see you going home with two girls. That's some playa shit."

"Man, I didn't even know they were like that though. For real!" I said, and then told him it was the pills that got them moving like they did. He seemed interested in the pills 'cause he had popped pills too, so I gave him my last pill, and he was like, "my man! That's what I'm talking about!"

I tell the dude my nickname. "I'm B.D. Melvin," and then I said,

"These girls are B.D. angels." We all laughed after that.

"It always went down like that in my neighborhood and in the clubs I went to. But I also had girls all out of state flying to meet me. I mean, I got so much money, I got a girl in Michigan, got a girl from Atlanta, and a girl from Minnesota. True story. I also had white girls, but I never really been into white girls, though. I had this one white girl, I only fucked her one time. It was a one night stand. We both had something in common, we both tooted raw, so I ended up fucking her for a day and a half after tooting together. I ain't seen her or talked to her since that day. She stayed in Kentucky. I fucked a couple more white girls, but I really don't mess with them.

"The girls I did mess with, they gave me so many problems. One time, my Uncle Pete saw me stressed out over a girl. She was special in a way, and pretty as fuck, looking like she was Puerto-Rican with the mixed skin color!

"What's wrong, nephew?" My uncle asked me.

"Man, this girl be stressing me out," I said to him.

"What's she doing to you?"

"This girl drove all the way from Chicago to Minnesota and put notes on my car, reported my ride stolen when it ain't stolen, and tried to get mad credit cards in my name and use them! She also text messages me and calls me 100 times a day! It got so bad, I called Verizon and got my phone service cut off, but this crazy bitch called Verizon and got it turned right back on! She did it just so she could keep in touch with me! This bitch should sign up with Puffy! She can't stop, won't stop!"

My Uncle Pete laughed for a few minutes. I knew he was about to say some slick shit to me.

"Nephew, don't let that bitch get you down! Don't change your life, change your wife!"

"I looked over at him when he said that, and you know what? I quit her the next day. He used to always say stuff like that to me. I always be exchanging funny lines like that with him. I came back to him one time when he needed help with one of his ladies and said to him, "you gotta be quick on your toes when it comes to these hoes."

10

BLUE HILLS OF CHICAGO

With all the women, sometimes it was hard for Melvin to stay focused on his occupation, despite Uncle Pete's quips. He was constantly choosing between his business or his pleasures.

"A lot of times, I was dope slanging so much that I wanted out of the game," Melvin said.

"It wasn't no secret or anything to my homies. I quit for like two years, or tried to anyways. I had so much money for two years that I just wanted to live. When I'm selling and gangbanging, I got pressure on me thinking that a muthafucka out there will someday come up with a better price or a better plan or even worse, money get so low with my customers I gotta back down like smack down on my prices. I always wanted to stop but didn't know a better way. And I think that's why I connected with rappers. People like M.J.G. and 8Ball were rapping all the time about what he can do to get out of the game. I mean, that's how I used to feel. Rappers talked about my life. Ain't nothing I don't think I been through they don't talk about."

Movies depicting street life also correlated to Melvin's

paradigm. In fact, some films seemed to be one step away from being a recorded version of the daily hustle in the Jeffrey Manor.

"I used to watch Menace II Society, Boyz in the Hood, the Wire. All those gangsta flicks. My movie though was Blue Hill Avenue. It was a gangsta ass flick about four dudes coming up in Baltimore. One is the hustler and the mastermind, the other one's the muscle, and the other guys cook dope up really good, and another one's a running boy, but it show how every muthafucka plays their position. It's only one motherfucking chief, only one boss in this clique and if they pay attention and everybody just does their part, things would go smoothly for them. And that's gotta go for anything, not just street life. That movie reflected my life and everything that was happening at the time."

One particular incident sticks out in Melvin's mind.

"I caught a dope case while partying in the nineties. I had a blue Bonneville with some blue tints on it and blue rims. The rims were the same color as the car, man. It was a '99 or '96 or something. I rode around in that car all the time. Well, there was this one day that everything was popping on the streets for me! I sold my buddy three eight balls, made a lot of money, and was just feeling great. Then the police pulled up on us out of nowhere and got ready to fuck with me and my partners. The dicks always be fucking with us too. So they searched my buddy, the one that I sold them eight balls to, and looked everywhere, even in his backyard for the drugs. They ended up finding the three eight balls and started asking us,

"Now, whose shit is this?"

"Man, I just stepped outside for fifteen minutes, where the fuck you get that from?" I asked them.

"Whoever got the most money, that's whose drugs these are going to belong to today," he responded.

"I was like, "DAMN!" I always kept too much money in my pocket, always carrying like sixteen, seventeen hundred on me at all times. That was the only dope case I ever caught. It all worked out but still this was something that always seemed to happen with me."

We was hiding out in the open, everyday with our Tanqueray, and making sure to stick our eyes up to the key hole, so we would be ready for anyone who tried to come at us.

I never thought I would need to watch my back.

Between every house is a pair of eyes staring back at me. Inside every home, I got a mirror that cracks when I walk by it. I used to just be a kid that played in the streets, and now I am a man who runs them.

11

I'M LIKE A CAT, YOU THROW ME UP IN THE AIR, I'MA LAND ON MY FEET

With so many incidents of police harassment, drug-selling gone awry, and friends turning into foes, Melvin wanted to at least experience the opportunities that his money could provide him. Namely, he wanted to experience a world outside the Jeffrey Manor. Melvin decided to travel and vacation as much as possible before something bad happened to him or his partners. By the time he was 26, Melvin was enjoying some of the best years of his life.

"I like to travel so I decided to try and go places I ain't seen before. Of course, I went down to Atlanta because I got family down there. I loved it too man. They had clubs that close at ten in the morning. They be serving breakfast in that muthafucka! I was so breezy! I ain't got an appetite by that time, but I would always order some water and orange juice and kick back and wait for the club to open again, and live it up! Atlanta was the place where you go to party. I know though if I lived in Atlanta, I wouldn't get nothing accomplished. It's too much partying and playa ass shit down there.

"I also went other places like Cancun and Cocoa Beach, but one of the best places I been to that tripped me out was Puerto Rico. I was really amazed by what I saw. The scenery was so beautiful. I was scared to get on the plane at that time, but my friend Big Homie, he went with me, he told me that "it ain't the planes that going to kill you, it's going to be the hood that does." I got off that plane and was all dressed in long sleeves, but in Puerto Rico, the temperature was 92 degrees! It was winter time back in Chicago, so we were laughing and feeling good the moment we stepped off the plane.

"It was funny too because Big Homie used to always cuff me under his wing. We already come together like night and day because he was a money-getting muthafucka. We used to ride together all the time. And so down in Puerto Rico, we had a Cadillac truck, and we were riding around in the Puerto Rican hood, and I realized Big Homie wasn't really prepared for doing business with them Puerto Ricans. So I had two 45's on me and put both of them bags in my back pocket. He jumped in the car, and I jumped in after him, then I jumped in the back seat, while Big Homie was driving.

"Man, why you in the back seat?" He asked me. And I think this is where the fact that he ain't a gangsta comes into play. We were on our way to sell some drugs.

"Cause when the muthafucka buying your shit jumps in the car, he's going to jump in the front seat and I already will have the ups on his ass," I told him.

"Big Homie slapped the dashboard. "Damn, you a thinking muthafucka, that's why I can never get your ass on anything."

'We got to the guy and where he stay's at, but the deal fell through. The buyer came to our window, we tell him to get in the car, but he trying to have one of us go into his place. I had to tell him that if he wants our product, get in the car, weigh that shit up, everybody will be happy, and things will be peaceful. But he didn't want to do it of course. I was like, "Big Homie, this muthafucka be playing games with us, he don't want to do this, let's bounce." So we got out of there, spent the rest of our time in Puerto Rico enjoying the weather and the beautiful girls that were down there."

Overall, Melvin's favorite trip was to the Bahamas. He had decided to treat himself, his brother, the girl he was currently dating, and his friends to a great time in the sunny island's plentiful sights and pleasures. "I had spent like ten thousand getting everybody to go to the Bahamas with me. I did it really big for everybody. 'Cause then the people with me will make sure I'm safe, and me and my loved ones wouldn't have any trouble. And from the time we left to the time we got back, we had a motherfucking ball. I mean, a limo took us to the airport, we flew first class, and at our hotel, it was all you could drink and all you could eat. I smoked some of the best weed of my life on that island too.

"When we got there, the first thing I realized was that it was super pretty. They had all type of exotic animals, just walking around all free. Big long-ass lizards, iguanas, and you could even take pictures with a pretty big-ass colorful parakeet. We had our own pool, everybody be taking pictures in the pool, and our own place I rented out. We took a ferry to the island as well, it was so nice. The ocean water was clear too.

"I remember we took a tour around that place, and my spider sense was tingling when we went by this one island in the Bahama Island chain, and I said to myself, man, they selling drugs on that motherfucking island right there. It wasn't five minutes later, when the tour guide said to us and said, "has anyone ever seen that movie Blow? That movie was based on the islands over there." I mean, that was one of my favorite fucking movies and here I am, right beside a place where Diego had made ninety million a week selling drugs. It was incredible.

"I also remember the first night on that island, we were at an outdoor bar and drinking and they were doing Karaoke singing. This white girl was snapping like a muthafucka! I ain't never seen it in my life! But the real kick was when she started singing "I like big butts and I cannot lie...!"

"We all just went crazy when she sung it. We started whistling and yelling! Those white people were really cool. I mean, I was used to white people holding their purse all the time around me. But they were on vacation just like we were on vacation."

Melvin returned from the Bahamas feeling closer to his homies and loved ones. It made him realize one of the most important things in his life was loyalty. He had to keep people close to him and never bring new individuals into his circle, for fear they might snitch on him or betray his trust. Concurrently, he also wanted to give back to the people in his community. He had seen so much peace while on vacation, he considered bringing some of those good vibes back home with him.

"I had my business set up pretty well and had this money to spend on my partners and family, but I wanted to do something good for everyone I knew back home. So I bought all the shortys their shoes for school. About twenty-eight, twenty-nine kids in all, and this was right after I got back from the Bahamas. I had won some money on the cruise boat gambling, like thousands. So I spent like three thousand dollars on the kids. I mean, three of those kids' mommas couldn't afford shoes for them or their mommas were on drugs. But these kids were little bad asses. They were cool. I like them if they're bad, but I don't like them bitchy. It sort of started out as one little bad ass kid saying to me, "I want some shoes!" And then before you know, the whole neighborhood was coming and asking me for shoes."

"I want some! I want some!" I heard them all yelling. It took me and my partners two days to do it. And Footlocker had a back to school special, buy one and get the other half off. It saved me some money doing this for the shortys. We took some out one day and took the rest out the next day. And it made me feel really good seeing the looks on their faces. And dudes were jealous of that, but it was for the kids, not for them. I can't tell a kid no. I mean, I made muthafuckas feel good. I also noticed the kids kept fighting each other while we handed out the shoes. So I bought them some boxing gloves next. Kids were using the gloves and fighting, so me and my best friend, we got to fighting each other with the gloves. I got him, he fell, but when I tried to wrestle him, he kicked the shit out of me. And all the kids were enjoying it and laughing. Afterwards, I gave all the boxing gloves to them and tried to educate them on how to fight.

"I always tried to be good to people around me. My mother used to say I got a lot of heart and always want to help people, like she does. That's our connection I guess.
"I think though, I had to finally put some money back into things for myself. So I opened up a vending machine company, and it's still going all right. But I ain't got the interest really in it. If I ain't got interest in something, I can't give it 110%. I was also thinking of opening up a Harold's chicken, but I wanted to write this book first to stop kids from killing each other. Another thing I tried was opening up a construction company. I had it for a year but it went away 'cause I had to pay taxes on it. I tried to rehab houses after that, but rehab houses were just a way of hiding my drug income. Of course, every dope boy's going to get a house and rehab it. The government pays you to do stuff like that and what could be better than this? But it only lasted for awhile. It didn't matter to me really 'cause nothing give me the kind of money like selling dope did.

"Even though I had put money into businesses and rehab houses, I also started putting up money. That's the one thing my momma did tell me,

"Put up something for a rainy day."
"And if I didn't do that, things would be fucked up.

I didn't really have any place I could trust though, so one day, I decided to choose somebody. I started giving money to my barber man. I gave him like fifty thousand to put up. Here I am, he cutting my hair, I got a gun on my lap, my head is tilted towards the door, and I'm watching the door, and on top of all this, giving him my money to hide. I mean, I was doing so much gangsta shit at one time, he got fired up at his barber shop. He still stuck with me though and we built a relationship and I ended up trusting him more than I trusted even my own dudes that were around me. I also helped him because of it. I gave him ten, twenty, even thirty thousand. He used to come over to my place and cut my hair, and when he did, he would see all the kis on the table, never say nothing. I trusted him so much I forgot how much time he had kept my money. I said to him one time, "thanks for holding my money these past two months."

"Two months?" He said with a surprise look on his face. "I been keeping your money for the past two years!"

"I knew I needed people around me like this. At the same time, I helped muthafuckas pay bills at their cribs, bailed guys out of jail, and hit muthafuckas that fucked with us on the streets. If I love you, I loved you. I've got a big heart. I mean, I even looked after this one kid for years. His name was Little Spike. His momma had seen me on the street one day and just drove right up to me, kicked his ass out of the car, and said for me to take care of her boy. She drove off and left me with her little kid. I guess she knew I was a guy who had money and took care of people around me. I was maybe 18 at the time, and this kid was only ten years old. I had laughed at first but then I realized his mother was serious. So I said, "fuck it." I took him in with me.

"Little Spike ended up being ruthless. He was another Yummy from our hood. This kid would be driving my car for me, but he couldn't even reach the gas pedal! He ran around and did my errands for me. He also had a spot at all of my cribs. Every one of them I set him up with his own room. Most of all though, he just liked to hang out with all the O.G.'s. He wasn't scared of them! In fact, a lot of gangstas were actually scared of Little Spike because he didn't give a fuck. He was super quick with a pistol. Had a great aim, knew how to use it when he had to do that. He grew up with me. And because I did this for him, he was loyal as a muthafucka to me.

"I had people like Little Spike and I also had people who I thought was friends but turned into foes. I think it's crazy though….I didn't even get a credit card 'til I was thirty-years old! I had people around me that have properties in their name for me, credit cards, whatever. This taught me that loyalty would take me farther than anything. I was loyal and kept it one-hundred with my guys all the time, and that's why we came out on top.

I told my homies, "they ain't never gonna defeat us, we gonna self-destruct ourselves." That's what would be the only way we could be taken down. But no matter what, I was like a cat, you throw me in the sky, I'ma land on my feet. If you believe, you will achieve. And with my partners, we achieved a lot because of loyalty and staying together."

That is, until wars broke out all around them, and their loyalty would be tested with bullets and bloodshed.

Melvin sat next to the club's front window, scanning the street outside for anyone who might be trying to creep up on him and his partners. The music thumped at a deafening roar and began to hurt his head. Or maybe it was the endless drinks served to him by friends who came to pay their respects. He had just got out of the hospital and was nursing an aching ankle. If something was going down tonight, he would have to stand his ground and unload his pistol until everyone was dead, 'cuz he couldn't run away if things got difficult. Not that it mattered to him. All he could think about was the cyclone of violence that seemed to whirl around him every day. It was like somebody had cast a voodoo spell on him in hopes that he would stumble into the path of a merciless buzzing bullet and he would be fatally stung. His breathing started to slip away from him just thinking about another hole being put into his body, but he quickly replaced that feeling of rickety panic with anger. Melvin's eyes became the color of fire, and anyone in the club who looked at him at that moment could sense his soul had merged with the devil.

Just then he noticed a beat up caddy accelerate fast past the club. It stopped just a block away and four tall men jumped out. "So that's them," Melvin muttered under his breath. He didn't want to alarm his friends just yet, but he was pretty sure these were the ones he expected to chop up the club with instruments of steel and death.

What these four assassins didn't realize is that Melvin would be ready for them this time. The entire club was filled with his homies. All of them were packing.

The four men prepared their assault. They jammed their hands into their pockets, no doubt to make sure their guns were cocked and loaded. Any minute now they would probably pull them out and run into the club and start shooting. Melvin noticed a tiny wind rustling through the row of trees across the street. Streetlights flickered and all the sound in the world suddenly vanished. Melvin knew what was next, but didn't flinch. The four men were at the club door. Melvin stood up.

"Let 'em come."

12

YOU GOTTA CROSS YOUR T'S SO MUTHAFUCKAS DON'T DOT YOR I'S

Around 1991, all hell had broken loose on the streets of Chicago. The G.D.'s went to war with the B.D.'s, causing them in many ways to break out of the Folk Nation and become a kind of new killing breed. Honor, turf protection, and control of the drug trade were responsible for hundreds of funeral processions in the decade that followed. In 1992, for example, 943 murders were committed in the windy city, and at least half of them from gang-related violence. By the time another century had begun, sobering statistics were reported by Chicago's police department which indicated that over half of all the murders in Chicago were done with a firearm, over 90% were committed by males, over 70% were done by African Americans, and over 70% of the victims were also African American. Yet all the statistics on gang violence and drug-related killings don't really mean anything. What matters is that a terrible precedent had been set in America. Namely, the reality of street violence equated to one unavoidable, horrific fact:

Black men were murdering other black men.

And when there's violence, there's a need for escape.

Thus, Melvin's drug operation was overflowing with customers wanting to forget the fact that stepping outside their home on any given day could be the last time they breathed air. Including for Melvin and his partners. The influence of belonging to the B.D.'s was, at first, something positive. Melvin had given himself protection in a mostly G.D. neighborhood. Yet at the same time, he wasn't immune to fighting or violence. It just seemed to follow him wherever he went.

"My crew and me whooped ass all the time. I mean, we're up against some real gangsta ass dudes, so we got to learn how to shoot and how to fight. I was in my Cadillac truck with three of my partners and we got into it with some dudes at the Lakefront. There was about twenty five of them and four of us. But we fucked them boys up real bad. Never cared about the numbers you know, I preferred twenty five dudes against the four of us. What I learned from living on the eastside was that I would rather have three solid dudes with me than ten chumps. I had confidence because I knew how good I was, and I would be able to whoop a nigga without him even being able to tell. But at the same time, I can go hard too. If a muthafucka had a gun on me, I'm still going to pull my gun out and be like, "Fuck your gun nigga!" People always tried to whack me but they really didn't want to play with me.

"The problem was that my lifestyle caught up with me. I was living like a fucking rapper. Like on MTV cribs you know what I'm saying? I mean, I had two houses before but I really liked the apartments better. I lived in one, had one as a safe house, and one where I cooked up my drugs. I even had one where I busted hoes down. I always had a lot of cribs. And I learned that being in the streets, you can't let your left hand know what your right hand is doing. Don't put your whole cards on the table. Gangstas will kill you for little or nothing just to get what you have. You gotta cross your T's so muthafuckas won't dot your I's.

"I had to live like this while coming up in an all G.D. neighborhood. It was at the time when war with them and just about everyone else was the reality. I mean, some sets were on our side."

The less the best.

"There were all sorts of different sets kicking up dust on the eastside. Goon Squad, Outlaw Boys, Boss Pimps, Terror Town on 75th, and the list goes on. They were all known for doing things in their own way.

"Still, I had to deal with problems all the time. I was selling the whole neighborhood, and I had to keep things under control. It got bad so bad there were sometimes two to three shootouts a day. I cook up a ki, take a lunch break, go shoot at my enemy's ass, go sell some drugs, and then head back to the kitchen for some more cooking. Police would make the block hot for awhile, so that's when I would give the block some air. Then I would go back and fire their asses up all over again. I didn't give a fuck. I would go to their houses. They couldn't rest.

"In fact, I was always good at finding where somebody

was staying at. My nickname was MTV Cribs. It's really a problem if a muthafucka come to your home. I would hit them at their home, then they would move and I would give them some time to unpack. And just when they were all moved in, I would come to their new place and start some gangster shit. I wouldn't shoot up their house though. It never did nothing to nobody. I would wait until a muthafucka stepped out to get in his car and go somewhere, then fire his ass up. I would chase them, and make them sideswipe the whole block.

"I wouldn't stop there though. I went to the clubs and fought people there too. I had the JMG Boys with me everywhere I went too, so I never really worried. Muthafuckas were nervous to hang out with us. One dude even said to me one time, "Melvin, I would go with you man to do a robbery or whatever, but you don't give a fuck about getting shot, so I know you don't give a fuck about me getting shot." I thought about it, and he was kinda right. I was getting into it all the time with people. It's Moes against the Folks, It's the Folks against the Folks, and so on. For example, Some Old G. guys had jumped on me, they were being lead by some Larry Hoover type cat, and him and his guys, they had their guns and had like ten or twelve guys on me. I'm only about eighteen, maybe nineteen years old, and this dude leading them is in his mid-forties. And what happened was, I had got into some trouble with this guy's son, who was a real disrespectful knucklehead, and we had got into an altercation where the son spit on me. So I smacked his ass. And the guy wanted to use this situation to start problems with me because he just got home from prison and didn't like what he was seeing. He did twelve years, and then he came home. Now, I am a B.D. and got the whole land on lock. So I'm fighting dudes with guns in their hands, and that's when I kinda realized that these people were nervous like my friend had been to be around me. These dudes were taking me serious. For them to come with all these guys and guns, I really got to be a problem.

"That's when I found out the worst thing about fear is fear itself. We fight it out, but they were as tough as me, acting like pit bulls when they see blood. Only one of them came up to me when it's done and said, "shorty, you a real dude, and I'm sorry for putting my hands on you." I highly respected that man, 'cause out of the ten or twelve O.G. dudes, he's the only one with common sense to see I'm a good dude that just wanted to do business. I made more money from hustling than anything else, not gangbanging, and I just wanted to make money to stay out of poverty. He's the only one I ain't try to get into it with whenever I saw them after this, but the rest of them it was on like a pot of neck bones.

"Of course, that wasn't the last time that set fucked with me. That's how it was in the hood. I was on my block, right down from my momma's house near the keyhole. Now, the keyhole was where I did most of my selling. We always liked this spot because most of the police couldn't really sneak up on us there. It was shaped like a keyhole. It's a cul-de-sac. So we could see the cops way before they could see us and got the advantage that way. They come up on us and we're gone. The only times we ever got it from them was when the cops got some party packs for

us. The party packs are when there's a group of guys and the police put bags of crack on every guy and locks them all up. But this time it wasn't the cops that fucked with me. This group whose leader was that old G., they had followed me from the keyhole one day down to my momma's place. I was outside talking to my mom and they jumped out of the car and started talking shit. I waited 'til they got close and told my momma to watch out. One of them walked straight up on me and I put my pistol in his face. I was about to kill him right then and there. My momma got between us, trying to make it all stop."
"We come to holla at you," the dude said.

"You don't come to holla at me at my mom's house!" I yelled at him.

"Before you know it, we were hearing sirens and the police coming. So my mother told us, "y'all go in the house with them guns."

"I ran inside and to make my mom happy, but told the dude, "You can come in my house to hide from the cops, but you gotta give me your gun. Ain't nobody going to be strapped in my house but me. Now, if you want to run that way, go ahead, but if you want to come in, I'm disarming you."

"So he gave up the gun to me, and when we was standing there, staring each other down, my momma got down on her knees beside us both and started praying. The dude then tried talking to me."

"The only reason I'm not going to kill you is because your momma's right here."

"I didn't say nothing, 'cause honestly, I would have shot him first if my momma hadn't been in front of me. I didn't give a fuck."

Melvin didn't always wait for the fight to come into his neighborhood. If he wasn't searching out his enemies at their home, him and his partners would roll around neighborhoods as a warning to other sets looking to make a move on the 95th crew. A lot of sets on the eastside of Chicago were scared to roll into other neighborhoods, due to the threat of retaliation and an increasing police presence. Indeed, speed bumps were placed strategically by police in all the hoods, along with eerie blue-light anti-crime cameras placed high atop of buildings and phone posts, but this would not deter Melvin's entourage from their mission. Not even the police themselves.

"Police got a job to do, and I got a job to do. I'm against those bogus ass police, ones that just fuck with me because they can. This one police officer though, I respect him."

He was like, "I ain't ever put shit on you."

"There were times I would get stopped, have to give police guns, and then they'd let me go. But honestly, I ain't upset at the police because it wasn't white cops shooting at me all day, it was black people shooting at me all day. And I was shooting back."

13

HOOD DOCTOR

One day, bloodshed had forced Melvin to become a hood doctor. "I saw most people die from bleeding to death, not from getting shot. I had to save people sometimes when they got shot. Me and my partners were chilling at this lounge club, and the place was filled with people. Next thing I know, gangstas started shooting the place up. I was right by the window when the bullets came through the glass and also through the walls. I couldn't see who was shooting either, but I knew they were using a chopper (i.e., an AK-47). I always used to wonder why they called it a chopper until I shot one. Every shell that came out, it would make a chopping sound, like, chop! Chop! Chop!

"So anyways, Boss Pimp Brian and my partner Curtis Blow and me, we on the ground. I got my gun in my hand in case the muthafucka who was shooting appeared at the door, and I'm going to fire that ass up. Suddenly my buddy Little Larry, who was also with us jumped up, and everyone else ran outside behind him and started shooting, and I was right behind him too. He was getting off so good, I let him have his night. I did manage to get off about two shots, but had to stop because there was too much action going on. Everybody else was now running behind me, everybody got their thumpers in their hands. But then I look over and see this Mexican girl, she crying and hollering, and completely covered in blood, lying right by the door. It wasn't the first time I had seen somebody shot, and certainly wasn't going to be the last time either. And the way she was panicking, it looked like she was about to die. I can tell when somebody's about to die or when somebody ain't going to die. I never did find out what happened to her.

"On my other side, a buddy of mine was shot up pretty bad. Blood poured out of him like he's getting an oil change. Or like he's a pig at a slaughterhouse. And he just slumped over and you can just see it in his chest where he was shot at. He's also bleeding too motherfucking bad to wait for an ambulance. So when it seemed safe, we drove him to the hospital. I applied pressure to the bullet wounds so he didn't bleed to death, but his intestines was hanging out, and I just stopped for a minute and pinched them. They were squishy and I was like, "eeewwww!" It was soft and gummy like some gizzards or something! But I pushed them back inside and hoped that could help stop the bleeding. We got him to the hospital in like two or three minutes, and he lived. Later on, I found out that those bullets were meant for me, not him. And you know what this fucking asshole was upset about when he's lying up in the hospital? He thinks I took his .45 gun off him when we were transporting his ass to the hospital! I didn't even touch his gun, somebody else took it at that time! I saved his life, and that's the thanks I got."

14

JUMPING THE BORDER FENCE

Melvin didn't find out who his attackers were, but it wasn't really a secret anyways. His B.D. status made him a prime target for bloodthirsty G.D.'s or other B.D. sets looking to usurp his throne. However, skirmishes sometimes occurred between his set and gangs from the Latino population in south Chicago.
"Latinos be existing mostly past 103rd st. It was like the divider. I grew up around blacks and Mexicans so it always was a beef thing between us. This one Mexican dude always used to fuck with me. I don't know what happened to him, maybe he fled to Mexico or something 'cause I know he was wanted for murder. But anytime I saw him, he dropping the forks at me. I ain't a G.D., but to him, if you black, you a G.D, and you ain't Mexican, so it was "D.K. bro." That's what he used to spit at me. And it seemed that I would run into this dude whenever I was with my big brother. One time, me and my older brother and his lady friend was all going into a neighborhood restaurant named Heiney's, and he come up to me out of nowhere."

"What's up Folks?" He said.

"Nothing," I replied. Then he continued more.

"What's up? What you on today? D.K. bro."

"That's some disrespectful shit. D.K. stood for "Disciple Kill," an obvious reference to who I was and how he wanted us all dead. I warned him and said, "If you don't get your gangbanging ass out of here, we going to light your ass up dude." But then my brother cut us off and he just laughed at him and said, "every time we see you man, you gangbanging on my little brother, why you keep doing that?" He look my brother straight in the face and said coldly, "'cause I'm a fucking gangbanger, bro!" What he said was really funny to me, but I was still going to set him straight. I was getting ready to bust his ass in the head with a 22 round, but then the police pulled up. I was ready to fight but the police weren't tripping about it. They told me, "we already know this dude is a jerk." I mean, it was always either Mexicans against blacks or blacks on blacks, and it wasn't the last time for me with the Mexicans either."

Melvin, Rhonell, and his little nephew had been walking down an alley near the "Mexican Border," which was the dividing neighborhood between all the south Chicago ghettos and a predominantly Mexican neighborhood, when a firefight erupted unexpectedly between a Latino gang and his entourage.

"My nephew at the time, he was talking with me and getting loud, and I had just got back home from visiting Atlanta, and was feeling crazy. We passed by this group of Mexicans who were standing on a porch. One of them suddenly yelled, "shut the fuck up!"

"I yelled back, "Who the fuck you talking to?"

"It pissed me off, so I hurried up and dropped my little nephew off and then me and Rhonell came back. I went up to the Mexicans and said, "I don't know how y'all talk, but we don't get down like that. Y'all better check things."

"I had my .45 and Rhonell was carrying his thumper, so we was ready. One of the Mexican dudes got off the porch and came at me."

"What you sayin, bro? What up?" He said.

"What up? What you wanna do?" I answered him. The tension began to escalate. We exchanged words back and forth. And while we were arguing, more and more Mexicans came off the porch and out of the house. I found out later they were having a gang meeting, so that's why they were saying to us to shut the fuck up! If I had known that, maybe we would have respected it. But it didn't matter at this point. There was about fifty of them backing up the one arguing with me."

"What? What? What?"

"That's all I kept hearing, so fuck 'em! That's what. I started blasting. I emptied my .45 at them, and we trying to hit all of them, even the ones still on the inside of the house. But I couldn't reload, 'cause they unloaded on us."

Boom! Boom! Boom! Pew! Pew! Pew!

"That's all I can hear. Me and Rhonell both start running. I wasn't even paying attention, and we run through some fields near the alley, ran to a car we had waiting. Rhonell came over the roof shooting back at those Mexicans."

Boom! Boom! Boom!

"He got them off me. I said to myself, Whoah, that's my nigga if he don't get no bigger! And we jump in the car, hitting it, and got about two blocks down when I felt something leaking down my leg. I didn't even know I was shot. So my partner took me to the hospital."

"Damn, I'm hit," I said.

"I got shot directly on my ankle bone. But then it started hurting. It was the only time I got shot that ever really hurt. Soon as I was seen at the hospital, the doctor took my shoe and sock off, and the bullet fell right out of my ankle. At the time I was really skinny, so it had went straight through. I was in the hospital about a week. I had my own room with a phone and television. And I filled it up with my partners, and made sure the Mexicans didn't come find me. I also sold dope while I was in there because my business wasn't stopping just because I'm banged up."

15

AM I THE DEVIL?

Although Melvin had been shot for arguing with the Mexican gang, the first time he ever suffered wounds from gunfire was on accident.

"I have been shot fourteen times in my life, on seven different occasions, and couldn't walk four times in my life due to gunshot wounds. I was twelve years old the first time I got shot. The dudes weren't even shooting at me, they were shooting at the group of guys I was with. I was so fucking young. I got shot in the leg, and I was scared 'cause I was hanging with the Boss Pimps and my momma had told me not to go over to 93rd where they was at. The ambulance came but I tried to refuse it. I was like, "nah, I'm cool, I'm cool, it ain't hurt." They gave me a shot and were trying to take me to the hospital. I still refused and told them, "Nah, just get me a band-aid or something. I'm cool, I gotta go home." But in the end, they forced me to go to the hospital and called my momma. I was trying not to tell her because she gave me that direct order not to go over there and I went over anyways with my buddies. They couldn't even do nothing to me 'til my momma came to the hospital so I had to wait and wait. I was watching Benny Hill 'til she came. When she finally did arrive, she cussed me out, and when I got out of the hospital, she was really strict with me for awhile. My mom was always stressed out about me. I never wanted her to know though, and it was funny because someone would come to the house and ask how I was doing. When she asked them what they meant, they would tell her that I'd been shot.

"I remember that first time, but another time that sticks out was right after I had got shot by the Mexicans. I was 21, maybe 22, at the time that happened. And I got shot again right after this incident. I threw a hood picnic. It was real pimpalicious. I was admiring my buddy's '96 Impala. It was painted a candy root beer color, but when the sun hit it, the car's body would change to like three different other colors. The interior had a cream veneer, and it was one of the first cars that rolled around on 21 inch rims. The Steering wheel was engraved with the Impala sign too. That thing was wetter than a baby's ass when it was in the tub! Man, paint can't get no wetter than that! We were all standing around the Impala, and my partner said, "the difference between men and boys is the prices of their toys."

"Getting shot that time at the picnic is kind of blurry. I mean, it didn't matter much to me. I remembered more about having fun at that party, not getting shot. However, it reminds me about this other incident where I had got shot six times. I was at my buddy Repass, drunk as hell, and off my square. I was fighting at the time with some muthafuckas, but I ain't expect them to come at me. They caught me with my guard down. It just goes to say, there's only one rule in the hood:

the trigger. I think to myself, what the fuck is wrong with me? I'm drunk, I'm almost dead. And the other guy that was fighting, he was trying to follow his partners out the club."

BLAM!

"I somehow got my fingers to work again and I shot his ass. The bullet spun him around, and he was lying on the dance floor with his head bleeding really bad. I shot his ass again. Now he's howling and moaning." "Shut your bitch ass up," I yelled at him.

"Big Fred grabbed me and said, "come on shorty, we gotta break."

"Before I left, I gave his ass one more shot.

"I come out the club while everybody is still running out of it. I was holding my side, but people thought I got shot in my legs 'cause I was bleeding so bad down my legs. And I never forget, soon as I get to the car, I fall right in front of them. My gun fell beside me too. Big Fred picked me up, grabbed my gun, put me in the car, and headed to Christ Hospital. I was shot in my ribs and my back. While I'm in the car on our way to the hospital, I felt sleepy, you know. I start to nod off, but Big Fred's smacking me, like, "shorty, stay up."

"My eyes are closed and I'm like, "It's cool man, I'm just kinda tired, I'm gonna take a nap."

"Suddenly, blood starts pouring out of my mouth. That's when Big Fred panicked, like, "oh shit, shorty bleeding out yo' mouth."

"He got to shaking my mouth, and blood's coming out and he's like, "Damn! I seen this on Menace II Society!"

"I had got shot in my lungs. I tried some more to go to sleep, but he smacked the shit out of me. I think he busted my nose he hit me so hard! It woke me up though. "Hey man, don't hit me no more!" I yelled at him.

"When we got into the hospital, I fell to the ground and it was crazy 'cause there weren't no people at the front desk. I was on the floor of the hospital for about ten, fifteen minutes. My partners had to go get the fucking nurses."

"This boy right here's dying, coughing up blood!!!"

"People got to running out, nurses and doctors or whatever the fuck they was, I really couldn't see anything. My eyesight was kinda foggy. And all I know, they put me on one of them beds with the wheels on it and I kept hearing, "we're losing him." I'm looking around like, what the fuck? Thank God there was this one lady, I don't know who she was, but she worked there and was like, "baby, everything going to be all right. Don't worry about it."

"I don't even give a fuck if I die," I mumbled between gasps of air.

"I really didn't even give a fuck if I die, but the lady just smiled at me and said, "oh, baby, don't talk like that," and just kept trying to comfort me. The fucked up part about it, the lady had put something on my forehead that burned real bad, and I shouted at her, "what you doing? That shit burns! Don't put that on me."

"It's holy water," she said.

"My condition now is all fucked up. And I know they have that thing on my face and kept squeezing it, and I was like, "stop that! Y'all taking my air! You keep crowding me! Give me a second!" I started blabbering my goodbyes to all my loved ones. Then I was knocked out.

"At this time, my whole family came to the hospital, it was that serious. They even had a priest do the last rite on me. My momma, she stood over me, saw me with all that blood, and her sisters, brothers, and mother were all there too. They tried to give me support. I woke up in another hospital the next day on life support. I had survived, but I wasn't even breathing on my own. I had a tube down my chest, had a tube in my nose. They had cut me open, trying to get the fluid out of my lungs, so there was a tube coming out of my side. I had these bag things on my legs and I had a catheter and an I.V. as well. I was fucked up. A little later after that, they took me off the life support, and I looked around and didn't know where I was. I tried to touch my face but I couldn't at all. I thought I was cuffed to the bed. I thought to myself that I must have killed that dude so they cuffed me to the bed. I had seen him bleeding out his head, and I thought I was the one who did that to him. I started ripping tubes up out of me, and my momma told me later I was restrained and then passed out again. I don't remember it though. I think that's the first time my whole family realized I was truly a gangsta and there wasn't any use talking to me. I wasn't a baby no more. Usually, my momma's like, "Melvin, you need to calm down or you'll get this or you'll get that," but after this happened to me, she was like,

"I can't tell you nothing no more."

"While I was recovering in that room, I remember there were a lot of people in my room the entire time. My momma there, along with every single one of my partners. Well, one of my partners found out that the dude I shot in the club...he was in a room about four or five down from where I was at!!!"

"Melvin, y'all on the same floor, we're gonna go fuck this nigga up!" My guys were livid but excited to have a chance for revenge.

"I guess my partner had accidentally gone to the wrong room and saw this dude lying there. So he went back and told me and everyone else. They wanted to get crazy up in the hospital, but I had to stop them.

"I warned them, "don't you know there's cameras all through this motherfucking place? You in a purchase-ass community. Y'all on a suicide mission, you going to be locked up until two thousand and forever!"

"If that wasn't enough, the pain really started hitting

me about two or three days after I woke up from being shot. I started hitting the button for some more morphine as much as possible, and it was banging!

While I was in a lot of pain, about twenty motherfucking police officers come in my room in the wee hours of the night. And the police were mostly homicide detectives. When they tried talking to me, I hit the button, like it musta hurt to talk with them. I just wanted them to leave me alone, but I really was in a lot of pain. My mom told me that the police had come in and tried to fingerprint me for gunpowder residue while I was asleep. They did it on my right hand, but I was shooting with my left hand because my right side had gone numb after getting shot. And a doctor had come in, seen what they was doing, and told them, "y'all gotta get up outta here, this is against the law to be doing this shit." And I guess they left or whatever.

"It was a good thing because soon as I got healthy enough to think straight, I was selling drugs at the hospital, like the other times I got shot. It was back and forth. It was kinda funny, I be doing business, then getting the morphine and falling asleep with ten thousand dollars in my hands.

"The one nurse in charge of me, she woke me up the first time that happened, and said to me, "baby, you have so much money on you! I never seen anything like that in my entire life! I put some covers on you so nobody see's that money!" That happened a lot, actually. I took the morphine and fell straight asleep. I needed to recover fast. All I was concerned about at that time was getting back to my business. When

I was discharged, they wanted me to stay inside the house for awhile so I wouldn't catch pneumonia. The day I got out of the hospital, I was back out doing my thing on the streets. And I didn't get into it with the muthafuckas who shot me right after I left, but anytime I saw them, it was on. We got into it again and again. I even got shot up a few more times as a result. But it didn't matter to me back then.

"You know, I think about getting shot in that club, and my momma not being able to really get through to me, but most of all, I think about that lady who put the holy water on me, and I wish I could have seen her again after that happened. I told her, "I hope I die, I'm tired of getting shot up, I don't care if I die," but she comforted me and let me know everything was gonna be all right. She must be a parent. She gotta have kids. She ain't know nothing about what I do. She just cared about my soul. She knew I needed Christ, but when that water burned me, I wonder if she thought I was the Devil. I wonder if I was the Devil. It would be awhile before God came into my life, but at that time, I wonder if God was trying to tell me something. Maybe God kept shooting at me, I kept getting shot, so then what? That's when I think God started to take everyone away from me that I loved, so maybe that would open up my motherfucking eyes."

We won the battle, but everybody lost the war.

Eastside Crazy

I heard the shots and fell to the ground
Damn another round
My friends really ain't my friends
My enemies are looking
More and more like my homies
See these fools they don't really know me
I'm surviving every time the shots
Rang and rang
But I'm still not out of time
It's worst than dropping a dime
It's not the cops
that keep pumping me with rounds
Been out less than two hours
My car got blasted like a cop on break
Holes through the door
Car spinning around
like my wheels is doughnuts
And as I swerve I find myself falling
Deeper and deeper into a state of "if onlys"
If only I hadn't start slanging
If only I knew the good seeds from the bad ones
If only I hadn't been there
Just sitting in that car outside that spot
Where they busted the door in
Sitting in this cell I'm feeling more than lonely
I'm feeling more and more angry!
Like life is passing me by
and no matter how high I get
I feel that pit of disgust in my
stomach that only makes me
Pray to the HOLY of HOLYS!
Are you there God?
Do you hear me?
I'm crying on the inside
And two weeks out of the hospital

Eastside Crazy

I'm locked down again
Damn I can't win!
I can't hold this plate man
Can somebody extend a helping hand?
But I'm in the wrong place...
See all the cats that feel this space
Have been through the same shit as me
So why would I think
They'd give a fuck about me?
More shots
More time
I'm standing but I can't walk
I feel a tingle in my throat
But my lips won't part
I can't talk!
I can't speak
I'm too weak
Because in my mind
I'm wondering if I could rewind time
Go back to a place
Where my mind wasn't in such a state of panic
of frenzy
The paparazzi I get is not friendly!
It's like the ghost of Christmas past
And my life looks like
It's ending in a casket
One more shot
And it might be my last 'g'
I'm feeling less than friendly
No one around to tell me it's ok see
Because they all walked away from me
So I can only look to Thee
Father can you hear me?

Alicia Williams

16

SOMEBODY'S GONNA GET KILLED TODAY

As the nineties dissolved into the new century, violence remained consistent and deadly in the streets of southern Chicago. Gangs had not ceased their destructive habits and consequently boosted the homicide rates to unknown highs. Death was a frequent visitor to the windy city, and often came at the end of a gun.

Despite this, Melvin had safely navigated his way through being a young teenager growing up on 95th St. to claiming the Jeffrey Manor as his domain in the drug world. His gang, the Black Disciples, had suffered consistent losses to their ranks due to constant pressure by rival sets and gangs, and especially the pressure from the overwhelming number of Gang Disciples surrounding them on every corner. Melvin persisted with his set to overcome shootings, drive bys, and jail, all the while remaining alive and in business.

Yet all that changed in less than a few years time, when an intense surge of gang warfare would forever change Melvin's perspective on his life.

"My dream team crumbled," Melvin said. "It was

Eastside Crazy

like every two or three months, somebody else died. Dudes I truly liked and loved, and even called my brothers. Some I looked at like they were my own personal kids.

"For example, when Suga Free died, I had just been with him right before he got killed. We were all at that club and he decided to go home, but me and my partners stayed at the club and did our thing. I couldn't believe when I heard he got shot in the back of the head, and then the guy took his gun and shot him 18 more times!

"Along with this, I had gone to Atlanta to pick-up a car I had left down there while visiting friends and relatives. While I was gone, I had left Little Matty in one of my big-ass cribs. It was a five bedroom house, several thousand square feet, with big flat screen T.V.'s, and plenty of drinks for him and my partners to have fun with. I also left them thirty poppers with clips. I told them while I was away to fuck off all weekend and take it easy. We hung out for awhile before I left for Georgia and I had said goodbye to him right before I left. But when I got to Atlanta, I got a call saying Matty got shot. He wasn't nothing but nineteen years old at the time. Little homie was a gangsta to the very end. After that, Baby Huey was killed, then Big Homie, and then Big Fred."

Everybody.

"I was waiting to get killed next. Seven of my guys got murdered in the space of a year and a half, and all on different occasions. This stressed me out, but all the times I got shot, it never really fucked with me. All it did was make me more angrier and upset. I raged a lot more too. I became cold-hearted and began to disappear inside. But when my set disappeared around me, and I was pretty much the only one left, it fucked me up real bad."

Death didn't stop there. Melvin and his friend A.C. had both been shot in a drive by.

"Me and A.C. were always money makers, but he was more of a hustler than anything. The problem with him was that he always was getting locked up. I never understood why he went to jail so much as clever as he was! He did like three bids in his life. A.C. was definitely the smart school type, played basketball good, and taught me about family. He would always take care of my family. So many times he would grab everybody's kids and head to Chuck E. Cheese. I tried to always keep him and his family right too. I mean, he'd call home from the joint and I would get him a care package, T.V.'s, a couple hundred on his books. I paid my ties. I've got to do this because you never know, I could be locked up any moment. Or killed."

"The day A.C. got shot, I told him, "somebody's going to get killed today."

"I've always had instincts like a prowling tiger. I can sense danger. Every time I had gotten shot, I said to myself, "don't go outside today, you'll get shot." But I didn't listen ever and this time it cost me a lot.

"A.C. was out of the joint and we were together driving around on some business. We had stopped and a car pulled up on his backside. I knew right then they were going to do something because for us to see who it was pulling up, we would have to turn around and that would give them time to shoot. It was smart because it gave them more safety and we wouldn't have a good shot out, when we returned fire. Sure enough, I was right, and they started blasting away at me and him in the car.

The driver was shooting at us and somebody in their car had two guns and was shooting them both at the same time as well. The very first shot hit A.C. in the back of his head. He had a frozen look on his face so I just thought he was in shock. I managed to grab my gun and shoot back, but it was bad. Bullets were everywhere, just flying into the car. I had to shoot out the front window so I could have a better chance to hit them. I let like eight rounds fly. It was around then I got shot right in the mouth. Blood flew all over, along with the broken glass, and there were smoke and shells everywhere. Then it was over. I had survived, and I thought A.C. had too. He was still breathing, but unconscious. The cops came and couldn't believe we survived though. The car was filled with bullet holes, and every window was shot out. The cops asked why it was so bad that I had to shoot out my own front window, and I just told them to talk to my lawyer. Actually, I couldn't really talk at all. My mouth was lying on the floor of the car. My lip was split pretty bad by a bullet.

"So I went to the hospital and got stitched up. I had around 29 stitches in my mouth. And while I was at the hospital, the doctors told me my dude had a bullet fragment in his head. It didn't seem good.

I waited for him to pull through, I mean, we all did, but he was lying in bed on life support and the doctor had declared him brain dead. His momma had no choice but to let him go. I remember standing there looking at him, and watching the oxygen pump slowly stop moving up and down as the plug was pulled. His tongue was hanging out the side of his mouth and tears had dried up while rolling down his face. I seen a lot of people die, but I ain't never seen death set in like that for anyone. His life slipped away right in front of me. Beep, beeeeeeeeep, beeeeeee eeeeeeeeeeeeeeep......................"

"A.C. was dead because of me. I mean, that hit was definitely for me. A.C. was working with me and I fucked him out of his life because of what we were doing in the Jeffrey Manor. A.C. had been there for me, and I wasn't there for him when it counted. His family knew this too and was tripping at the funeral. Everybody in his family got their eyebrows up when I attended, but they didn't say nothing. To this day, I feel bad about that. I ain't never cried about nothing on these streets until A.C. died.

"What I went through with A.C. dying and my dream team disappearing, it wasn't normal for a grown man to experience. Muthafuckas would be somewhere with a straightjacket on, but it ain't about how you fall, it's how you get back up. I had to keep going. All these things had shaken me and I looked around and realized I gotta try to learn from my partners' mistakes and my own as well. One of my partners, his momma ain't got no more kids because both her sons died doing the things I was involved with. And A.C. dying made me angry and frustrated. Especially when I got convicted for having guns, and while I'm heading home from the court house, I've got my enemies shooting at me as soon as I get out of the court. And I don't got my guns on me yet. Somehow I made it but my other buddies, I mean my Stone buddy, his whole motherfucking set got killed. If we was in the Army, it was like his whole platoon got wiped out. Death came fast and took everyone all at once at the end of my reign in the Jeffrey Manor. "I think about how these kids coming up that kill somebody, they should be taken to the morgue and have to do the autopsies on their victims. They should sit there on the front line and see how many people they've affected, because I didn't realize how one person dying can affect so many people. Maybe then it would set in how much hurt can come from one action that could be stopped if niggas just settle shit like men instead of like babies with big egos and bigger guns. And who suffers the most when the shooting stops? It's always the family.

"One day, A.C.'s son asked me why his daddy's dead. I didn't know how to answer that, but then I decided to tell him the truth: because they were trying to kill me. How could I have let this happen? I started really thinking that there's gotta be more than dope dealing and killing. And hearing A.C.'s son ask me that question, I decided to change my life right then and there."

Melvin picked glass out of his hair and face. His upper lip was split in two from a bullet that tore through it, and blood spurted out of the gaping hole in his mouth as a result. The car engine continued to softly purr while being pushed into park. Melvin couldn't really hear anything at the moment though. All that filled his head was his own screams and the brief shouts from A.C. right before a bullet was lodged in the back of his brain. It had been a standard ambush set up with his enemies rolling up on them from behind and unleashing wave after wave of gunfire into the car. Melvin was able to fire back a few shots, but he had been thrust right into the middle of a gun battle maelstrom. When it was over, he had somehow survived, but his best friend was now lying in the hospital stuck in critical condition.

Critical condition.

Permanent condition.

Death.

Melvin tried to sit down on the curb while the police asked him questions. The fountain of blood on his face continued to gush everywhere. Soon the paramedics would arrive to help him, but until then, he would have to just wear shock for a band-aid. Melvin dumped his head in his hands and rocked back and forth on the ground.

How did it come to this?

17

ONE LAST STOP ON THE ROAD TO HELL

On April 20th, 2008, Chicago newspapers all shared the same headline: "32 shot, 2 stabbed, 9 dead."

It had been a weekend of brutal slayings by gangs over the entire city of Chicago. Over 20 people alone were shot and nine killed between Friday and early Saturday morning. There was so much killing going on that a few years later, the mayor of the windy city started calling it "Chi-raq."

During this time, Melvin was busy preparing for a business trip to St. Louis. It had been two years since A.C. died, but the decision to change his life hadn't set in yet. Walking away from the life he lived would be tricky and was going to take some timing. Until it happened, Melvin continued with business as usual.

Before he took off for St. Louis, he had planned to meet his "little" cousin Naton (who was 18) and his best friend Volts at the Free Salvation Methodist Baptist Church on the 7500 block of South Phillips in Chicago.

"Naton and Volts were robbing people. They were

terrible with it, but I loved them. They used to punk me all the time for money. I give them twenty dollars and two hours later, they be back asking me for another twenty!

"Anyways, I wanted to meet up with them before I drove down to St. Louis and I was on my way to meet them. I was on Martin Luther King Drive and my little cousin kept calling me. I was like, "bitch, quit calling me so much. I can't get there no quicker!" "Okay bitch, but hurry up!" He said.

"My little cousin, that was the type of person he was, and when I would cuss him out, he would talk shit to me, but in the end I was always, "aight, cuz, I love you man." My cousin wasn't no killer or anything, just cocky. Him and Volts was trying to do things they saw us older guys doing.

"So I pulled up to the block they were on, and saw police cars and an ambulance, and I parked my car down the street and crept up to see what was going on. It turned out, Volts and my cousin were standing in front of a church when somebody pulled up and shot them dead. Naton had been hit in the neck, and Volts had been shot in the chest and back. Right on the porch of that church. There was nothing they could do. They were gone.

"Me and the older guys, we was so busy doing our own thang, we didn't pay attention to Naton and Volts. If we had paid attention, we would have seen that they were trying to be like us, and maybe we could have been better role models for them.

"I started really thinking about change again. My friend A.C. got killed and now this? I had lost everyone. It was strange, but since Naton got killed and A.C. too, I grew closer to my mamma. She never agreed with what I did though. I had to up guns on dudes in front of my ma. I really tried to stay away from her so I wouldn't bring harm her way. But now every day we started talking and seeing each other. The fucked up part about it though is that my grandma and the rest of my family told me that they really thought it would be me that got killed, not A.C. or Naton. And it didn't hurt when they said that, but I know my momma wanted me to be right. She prayed for me every day, going to Apostolic Church of God in Christ and making sure God was watching over me. I don't know if my guys went to heaven or not, and I didn't care about getting shot or killed, but my momma always looked after me in her own way. She had a stroke and made it through, and then her and my neighbor prayed for me! Her neighbor thinks I'm going to be a minister, and I really think maybe I'm alive today because of her faith. That could have been me on the porch with Naton and Volts if I was just a few minutes earlier."

Eastside Crazy

Warm weather leaves more than 30 dead!
That's what the paper read!
Blaming the weather on crimes that are cold and
heartless!
These niggas is wearing gloves
and their souls are arctic!
What's temperature got to do with the
state of mind these young niggas Is In?
After they leave home after they've done time?
It's like a ticking bomb...
hidden in the concrete jungle!
ONE OF THEM LIL NIGGAS WAS MY CUZN!
Shot dead at the age of 18, lying on the steps
of that church that read "Free Salvation!"
Can you imagine taking your last breath on the
steps of a place that's Offering free salvation!
Moments of mediation, these
shots were pre-meditated!
The evil plans of the devil as
he walks through the hood!
That nigga always up to no good!
I should've told them to wait, I should've
told them a different route to Take!
One last breath one last word...was their eyes
opened when their souls Reached heaven's Door?
The weather ain't got shit on my
block cuz that mutha fucka is hot!
These streets are crazy!
Running for your life while
standing on the corner hustling!
Every day is the same ol shake and bake!
I'm dying to live and while I
live I'm gon' take and take!
I got to take more than I give,
sometimes more than I make!

Eastside Crazy

I get locked up, I get out just,
to get locked down again!
These gangs is crazy, and that's why I
get high and my mind stay purple Hazy!
They like to think that we dumb niggas and lazy!
But these gangs is always on the
grind and they killing our babies!
I'm caught up in the middle
of the whole shebang!
The money, the power that fucked up street fame!
Selling dope to that lil kid's Pops!
He sat and watched as he shot and
pushed that shit right into his veins!
Getting caught in this rotation
of drug crimes and probation!
Being the best at what I do, but then too, I'm a
part of that disciple Nation That don't like to wait
for shit cause it ain't patient!
And neither is the other side, they
down for they set and they ride!
Guns blazing, in that neighborhood where my
cousin and his friend was Walking!
Open fire that rang through
the street like a bell in a tower!
The neck, the chest, and the back!
It was just 2 of them and they was under attack!
So there lies their inevitable end!
This life just sends you sin after sin!
Creating a whirlwind of lost kids!
Young mothers, baby daddies instead of fathers!
Some girls getting pregnant
and saying why bother!
And the spot it stays hot!
That's why week after week these
lil kids keep getting popped!

Eastside Crazy

*So what they saying, the
weather is making em crazy?
It get hot they got guns and then
what, they go out shooting for fun?
So it's the 4th of July, every
winter, spring and fall!
These niggas is north, south,
west, and eastside crazy that's all!
Living on the edge of a waterfall!
No tall grass to run through they
parents on dope so guess what?
The street is raising you!
That's what they want us to believe!
Not that they created a generation of angry seeds!
Growing from the concrete, trying to stay
above six feet selling dope so Our kids can eat!
Damn!
This shit goes beyond a warm sunny day!
It's time for us to kneel down and pray!
And hope that God really sees all and before
anybody else does He'll Catch Us before we fall!*

Alicia Williams

18

LOVE BIRTH

Throughout Melvin's life, women had always been attracted to him. His six foot, two hundred pound, muscular physique made him intimidating to members of the opposite sex, but his fast smile and slick charm branded him as a ladies' man. Indeed, most women had told Melvin that he wasn't exactly marriage material, but the kind of guy you want to have fun with and date. He had always tried to balance work with play, and with everyone around him getting shot up, including himself, life had to become something more than just living day to day making money. Melvin was used to taking care of his partners in the streets like they were his brothers, but thanks to his consistent playboy mentality, he ended up with kids bearing his genetic code, all to different women.

"I've got four daughters, and one son," Melvin said. "Tara is my oldest daughter, She 13 now, and was born when I was doing time in Division 11 at county. Keeva is my second daughter, she was also born when I was locked up in prison for two months. She's disrespectful to me, but I can't really chastise her 'cause her momma is an idiot. Keeva hear her momma talking bad about me and so she does the same. I ain't get mad. I just tell her, "don't talk to me like that, I'm your father." She tells me to "Sssshh!!" I would pick her ass up, like "come here! Get your ass in the room!! Time out!" She always say to me then though, "Okay, okay, I'm sorry daddy." But I had to do it like that because her momma let her get away with letting her treat me bad. She was always trying to turn my daughter against me. So I'm pretty sure there's going to be a problem with anything I say because of it. Having kids to all different women is one of the worst mistakes I have ever made. I had wanted all my kids to come from the same lady.

"Like Sherell, she's four, and I see her sometimes, but my youngest daughter, Neecee, she doesn't really even know me. My one son I ain't seen in a long time either. Maybe over a year. His mother didn't even want him in the car with me 'cause I was getting shot too many times and having too many shootouts. She told me I won't be able to see him until he turns 18! That ain't right. There are muthafuckas that don't give a fuck about seeing their kids and I got to threaten to take this girl to court just to see my son? But she does it to hurt me for not staying with her. Neecee's mom does the same thing to me. She won't let me see my daughter either.

"I had lived with two of the women that I got pregnant and it worked out well. I even took one of my baby's mommas to the Bahamas with me. But these girls are having babies for their own reasons. They think they came up on a lick or something. They want to get me on child support, which one of them do. I just don't see eye to eye with that woman. She's a selfish woman. When A.C. got killed, she mouthed off so low about it that I smacked her. Never put my hands on her or any other girl like that before but she crossed the line about A.C. with me. I had got locked up over what happened with my friend, and she still trying to take me to court! After I got out, she tried to scare me, telling me the police had a file on me as thick as the yellow pages! She told me, "the police really want you dead," yet she still wanted to press charges on me! I couldn't believe after everything that happened, she was going to go ahead and try to suck more money out of me and inconvenience me....what a spiteful bitch! But hey, treat people the way you want to be treated. To each his own.

"I'm trying to be a good father figure to them but it's hard. I really cherish the times I spend with my children though. I got good relationships with some of them, but I want to have great relationships with all of them. I had a house in the suburbs for awhile so they could come home and not worry about gangsta bullshit. I would have to move place to place because my enemies and police wouldn't find out where I live and I had to be smarter than that to stay in one place for too long. It was hard being the way I was and trying to raise kids at the same time. I had to look out for my kids and also my partners as well. I also try to play Uncle B.D. for Christmas and birthdays to my friend A.C.'s kids even. For instance, his son called and said he wanted five hundred dollars to buy a Playstation three. Somebody had broken in to his home and stole the one he was using at the time. I had just bought a Playstation three for Christmas but never played it, so I told him, "Tell you what. I got a Playstation three, and I'll just give you mine." He was so happy, and I try to be a father figure with him. I can't be no dad though, but at least I try to keep it one hundred with him and do my best.

"It's exactly the same with my oldest Tara. She know's I keep a gun and understands never to touch it, but she ain't got that mentality I got. I ain't worried about her being a gangsta, plus she's a woman. It's different for black males and black females. It's much harder for black males. I'm kinda glad I only got one boy. I'm glad I got all girls. And Tara, she's got my business senses, not my anger. Like, I got the wholesale rights for my vending machines and I say to Tara that she should learn how to do business with people and make money. She sold some stuff at school to her friends and came back and said to me, "look at me, I'm a hustler too, daddy."

"I just look at her and say, "yeah, baby, you ain't no hustler, shut up."

"Then she got this idea in her head she can use my vending machine service even more.

"Daddy, I tell you, I can sell some candy."

"Yeah, baby, you know what? Let's go somewhere."

"I took her to the outlet store and told her, "baby, I want to show you how to be a hustler. I bought a hundred and thirty-seven dollars worth of candy to sell to people. I bought it from the same place that grocery stores buy their products from, so it's like a better price. Now off this, you gotta go to the store with your money and the candy, and you gotta sell some."

"Now in three days, she came back to me and said, "dad, I got a hundred and seventy-five dollars!"

"Damn, baby, you are a hustler. Well, okay, how much you spent though?"

"I ain't spend nothing," she said.

"Well, you know, stack your paper. Your goal should be to stack a thousand dollars and put it in your bank account!"

"Then Tara's momma told me later on, "You fucked up with her Melvin. Now when we go out to eat, Tara be wanting crab legs. You know she going to be messing with the drugs and the boys 'cause her daddy got her crab legs. She ain't gonna want no cheeseburger and french fries.'"

"You know what?" I said, "That's all right if she wants expensive things."

"I went and told Tara, "If you want to be living large, you got your own bank account so you can buy your own crab legs. Don't depend on no man to support you!"

19

TIME TO UPGRADE MY PACKAGE

Watching his children grow up next to the violence that claimed most of his friends and family, Melvin finally made the changes necessary to keep surviving.

"One of my partners that made it, Pierre, he religious now. Sometime after my friend A.C. got killed, he asked me to visit his church in Indiana, so I agreed. When we were there, he spoke at the front of the church and then asked me to sit up front too. I don't even really remember what happened, but I let loose what was inside me and started preaching and feeling what the crowd was giving me back, which was appreciation for my words. Then his pastor put me on the spotlight.

"Son, have you been baptized?" He asked me.

"Nah, I never been baptized. My momma wanted me to get baptized one day though."

"So you want to get baptized today?" He said.

"I thought about everything I went through, and A.C. dying next to me."

"Yeah, I'ma get baptized," I answered.

"He said, "good! Come on and get baptized now!"

"Then I sort of panicked and didn't want to at that moment and told him, "hold on right there." But everybody started standing and clapping. So I said, "aw, damn. I guess I can't redo." I got baptized while my buddy Pierre watched.

"You know, the funny thing is, since I got baptized, I ain't angry like I was. Before this, Pierre had asked me, 'why you so mad at what you become when you worked so hard to get there.' I just looked at him shocked. So now, I ain't got that hatred in my heart. I had a temper problem, and I definitely don't like being around groups of people. I would beat somebody up even if they looked at me wrong. I didn't trust anyone, just myself, and kept my gun off safety.

"Now though, I want to forget about my paranoia and do some challenging things. I don't want to sell dope. Been doing that all my life. I mean, too good. Everything I'm weak on, I'm trying to work on. I'm weak on education, I'm weak on the corporate world. So I'ma try to get a piece of the stock market if I can. Being baptized was good for me for this reason. I have believed that there's gotta be a God upstairs that cares, right? And if God wants to teach me stuff, what can I lose learning from God? I'm just going to feel it. That's my instinct.

"I started to work out five times a week trying to

release stress. There's lot of things I want to do. I decided to work towards a more legitimate business route, besides what I already have with the vending machines or my potential investment in a Harold's Chicken. I wanted to do something that won't take me away from my kids. I seen so much death that I gotta change. It's like Who Wants to be a Millionaire, man. I ain't got no more lifelines.

"My Uncle Pete knew everything I went through and told me, "do what you gotta do, but you keep playing and doing unnecessary shit, you going to pay the price."

"He was right too, so I stopped doing everything in my life that wasn't necessary. For real.

"The problem was that I needed to get away from all the drug dealing. I had got some religion in my life and it helped control my anger, but I was surrounded by gangs and dope. So changing completely was going to be difficult, even after everything I went through. I was still selling kis, and was always saying how tired I was of doing it. I wanted a way out, and always thought maybe if somebody could have showed me a real way out, I would have quit. But even when I tried to quit myself, the game just pulled me back into it. That's when this gangsta bitch named Uncle Tammy who heard me complaining told me to "upgrade my package."

"She kept a 38 short nose revolver in her back pocket and liked the pussy as much as I did. Nobody disrespect her to her face 'cause the girl was good with what she did, which was slanging dope and shooting her enemies before they shot her. So I heard her words and really thought about them. I think I need to upgrade my life by replacing what I was going through right now. I mean, it's been raining past 40 days and 40 nights all my life."

CONCLUSION

"So I figured out what I really needed to do. One day, I was looking at the elections and watching President Obama speak, and he's talking about time for a change. I think what President Obama was doing was a beautiful thing. He helped me feel more comfortable just heading downtown into Chicago, making me feel less paranoid. This was the same time I got advice from Uncle Tammy. It hit me. The next day after watching President Obama, I grabbed a U-Haul, packed my belongings up, left it in the parking lot of my apartment complex, then drove up to Minnesota and looked for a new crib. I found one in a day, then came back and grabbed my belongings, and moved up there the following day. I needed to get out of the Jeffrey Manor. I went just me and nobody else.

"When I moved up there, I realized there were drugs here too, but I didn't need to be part of it. Instead, I checked into the possibility of becoming a chef. I loved to cook, so it felt natural to me that I would do it for a living. Along with this, I went fishing as much as possible. I really like the conversations that strike off fishing. Like, white people come talk to me in Minnesota. It ain't like that in Chicago. In my

Minnesota neighborhood, there's a black man down the road, then you got an Asian family living next to you, and next to them you got a white person. Across the street you got a Somalian. Next to them Africans, then another black guy, maybe. We all live together here and I love it. Every tree got a couple of bad apples of course, but a real muthafucka will see through that.

"I'm up in Minnesota, but I still gotta remember all my partners. I can't forget them. I had got a lot of tattoos on me as a reminder of who was important to me and where I come from. I got the names of Naton and Volts on my veins, so they be running through my blood at all times. Got the praying hands too. Been kinda stressed out, so I gotta have somebody to pray for me. That's a C. Murder rap quote:

"Somebody pray for me."

"My first real attempt to change things after everyone got killed and I got baptized I actually tried to do while I was still on 95th was with the construction company. I did it so I could get out the dope game. I felt like it was a new beginning for me, and I couldn't think of a name for my construction company so I named it for my dead partners, Matty, Suga Free, and A.C. I called it M.S.A. Construction. It ain't become too successful but I believed in it so I put it on me. This helped me to understand where I come from. I was blessed I didn't die, blessed I didn't spend a lot of time in prison, and blessed I didn't catch A.I.D.S. from fucking around so much. AND with all the dumb shit I did, like running up on a muthafucka with my gun to constantly getting into it with the

G.D.'s and other different gangs, I ain't NEVER gonna forget where I come from. EVER. I mean, I felt a lot and loved a lot and was loyal, but I realized my loyalty was to the wrong muthafuckas, and the ones that were loyal to me paid the price with their lives.

"I realized also that I never failed on nothing I ever did in my life. I just did the wrong things to get it. I think for a long time, I was doing the Devil's work, so now I'm going to see what it's like doing God's work. I made my own path, made my own way, and my partners we looked out for each other. However, when they were in jail or killed, ain't no muthafucka took a lollipop for me. I learned the rules of the streets, got my ass whooped when I was younger, I learned how to fight and survive in the jungle with my shoes off.

Now, I got a break and I'm trying to do right. I mean, everybody had a time in their lives to chill out from going to prison, even getting killed. Everybody had that break, and some people got a permanent break, and this is mine. I gave up control of my neighborhood and even though I could make one phone call and it could be on again, I'm just tired of it all. I had respect because there were many times I could have got revenge on people and shot them up, sent them away, but I didn't. I handled my business like a man does in my situation. So now I set up a peace situation in the Jeffrey Manor that I hope people are going to respect, but young kids come up and don't give a fuck, there's going to be trouble for sure.

"I think people need to get involved to stop people

like me from happening all over again. Everybody needs to get way more involved. Who are these kids looking up to? No one except rappers and gangstas. Churches, schools, all of us need to step in and try to help kids before it's too late. My idea is simple: do one good deed a day. Help a lady across the street, give some money to a poor person, or take time out to talk to your kid and help him with his homework. Get involved in a positive way. We've got so much hate in this world now, we don't see people doing good any more. It's going to have to get better. And it's not just a black issue. It's a people issue. My life I take responsibility for what I've done and am making up for it as much as I can.

I didn't choose the game, this game chose me. I can sit here and blame the man and all that, but the man didn't do nothing to me but give me options. I mean, a white muthafucka never shot me, it was always a nigga every single time. I put my hand out now, these are my cards, and I play my cards the way I have them. Everything I went through...it was gangsta, it was playa. It was love, it was heartache, and I wasn't just a product of dope who blamed everyone around him for his problems. I made things happen around me. I threw hood picnics, made sure the guys around me and kids are straight, and carried the whole weight of the neighborhood on my back. I turned men from chumps into champs. Yet those same muthafuckas would turn their backs on me, piss in my face and tell me it's raining. I ain't tripping though. I kept shining on, and I've been given a chance to do right in the world, so I'm gonna do exactly that.

"I was looking at some old notebooks me and my partners used to write in, talking about what went on in our lives, and I came across something from my friend A.C. He knew his life on this planet would end before he had a chance to grow old, and I think about these words and growing up on the eastside of Chicago. This was written not just with A.C.'s blood, but with my blood and everyone else who grew up there and knows what I'm talking about:

Eastside Crazy

So as u can see
It ain't no peace over east in the belly of the beast
Just let the truth b told
How can u love the streets
When the streets don't love you back?
The devil can't tell u that he loves u
Like true story

It's already 2 late 4 me
But thru my mistake u can learn from it
I can't come back
Don't make the same mistakes I made
1 thing 4 certain and
2 thing 4 sure
The hood is going 2 remember me
Through history
I never wanted 2 be the man
All I wanted 2 be
IS a man

Mama don't cry
I'm ok
I'm in heaven looking down on u
1 thing u must know
I didn't choose the game
This game chose me
And if you're reading this book
That must mean I'm dead
And the fucked up part about this all
I was killed by the hands of another black man

Damn.

Michael Colyar

DEDICATIONS

Dedicated to Melvin Thomas and Rhonell Savalas, and all those that lived and died in the Jeffery Manor, May you rest in peace.

Naton, Volts, Nuffy, Bo Mayon, Lasaro, Muhammed, Daveo, Oatmeal, Kansas City, Disco, Little Joe, Curtis Blow, Little Larry, Punkin A.K.A. Suga Free, Little Matty, Pier, Fred and Fred Jr., Pook, Shannon, Lorell, Herby, Savalas, Little M.C., Jerome, Pookum, Too Big, Ice Mike, BabyFace, A.C., Twon, Louie, Anna, Lil' Gutta, Majelin, Big Dean, Tara, Keeva, Neecee, Sherell, White Brian, Oscar, Elliot, Tyrone Bufkin, L.B., Skeeta Wheat, Chew, Boss Pimp Brian, booze, Marvin and Slick Rick.

Eastside Crazy

Now, if you think this shit isn't real, here are some letters from real people involved in my story. I've included their prisoner numbers and where they are being held at so you can see that when you live as I did and you think you've got the life all figured out, it could be you sitting in a jail cell for the rest of your life.

Eldrick Anderson
Prisoner Number R08335
Menard Correctional Center
Offense: Murder with the Intent to Kill
Sentence: 28 Years

This letter is to the future, I'm going to start off by Blessing the reader's and saying this isn't the place to be!! My name is Eldrick Anderson and my number is R08335 and when you in any correctional facilities, all you are is a number, the number they give you. Four out of ten times you all have heard the saying, "stay in school and say no to gangs." Okay, now that's true. A lot of inmates will tell you that they drop out of school because of gang's and yes drugs too! But we're not going to talk about other inmates 'cause most of them are fake, faggots, or pussies, misery loves company and a lot of these inmates are miserable. Some of your friends may have quit school and are out on the streets when you're in school.

Now at times it seems the fun thing to do, but you can go to school and finish it and the same people will be doing the same things if they not dead! The streets will always be there. Now when you get caught and go down, the hard part is watching your loved ones or so called family play you like you aren't shit! Few women help you in time of need. Family turns into associates and friends turn into a thing of the past. Now can you imagine your mom, children, and women dead, now that's pain but more pain comes when they not dead and act like you're dead. No help, no money, no pictures, and all you have are memories. Now when you're in these walls it's two ways it can go. Take something or get your shit took! And it's always laid back. Now you're in here with, let's say Five years and your cellie has 85 years and I got 30! Let's just say your family is helping you and sending you money. Now you have niggaz not going home. And if this home to them you in for it! Niggaz will take your shit every time you get something. Your cellie gets your shit one week and the next week I'm getting your shit too. This does not stop. Now we're getting to the point where we going to make you pay rent for protection. Now if you don't want to pay we're still taking your property, food, and all plus beating your ass the whole five years you're here!! Now just say you got five years and no one is sending you money, now how you going to get soap, you have to buy yourself a blanket, tv, fan, and lamp. Menard is called the pit and it has that name for a reason, it gets so hot you need two fans but you don't have even one!

The state is all soy meat and that's not good what you are you going to eat? You have no money, what about toothpaste? What you going to walk around with hot breath, no soap to wash up with? Then on top of all that the police tell you when you can wash

Eastside Crazy

up and go eat, you can't do nothing when you want to do it they tell you when to move! The state gives you $7.00 a month but that's only enough to get one toothpaste and one deodorant and one bar of soap, so make it last or sell your soul! Now, if you got to ask niggaz for soap, toothpaste, and food. Niggaz want something for something. Nothing for free! Might be that booty hole or you might have to kill someone for it, but just know that your booty can be bought for a dollar soap! And you will do what your told or you'll get that butt took or killed! Can't pay what you owe because you don't GOT nothing. So now you're someone's hoe and you know how niggaz do a hoe, they run up in a hoe. After that, you are now someone's property. People come down here with one year to do and sometime don't go home because they get killed and the one's that do make it out did more than a year by getting time on top of time by fighting! You have to fight in here for the little things and yes, we do have knives to kill your ass!

Then to top it off, you fighting people with A.I.D.S. that don't care and trying to give it to you, and make your time here longer. Like I said, misery loves company, and haters want to see you down and out! And I'm one of the blessed ones, but I have my bullshit days too! Now I'm locked up for murder and by me being locked up more than once, my murder started at 45 to life! But I wasn't about to play with them people's intelligence, plus I know I did and they got the evidence. So I copped out, yeah everyone I knew was mad at me for the move I made, but only one nigga is still here with me and that's RARE!

I thank God for him every time I think about him.

Loyalty and unity my brother! Fifty two hours and 32 days my nigga! But I know I have to do the time. I took 28 years instead of playing with the state, which they was trying to put me under the jail. I'm 28 and I got 28 years, I'll be 56 when I get out if I make it out. People die over seven dollars a month state pay, me I don't know how I'll make it. It's kill or be killed and the bad part is, I'm in here with the bullshit. The best thing is to be your own boss, get a career not a job, but a career in something you like doing and you'll be getting paid for what you love to do! You can't beat that! You'll be surprised how people act 'cause you out of sight and out of mind! Everything you need in the world you need in here, but with no help, you in trouble. It's hard to get out but easy to get in, trust me. You're in a five by eight cage, you and your cellie all day not only do you have to smell your shit but his too! And when you look the word cage up in the dictionary, it says: A box of wire or bars for containing an animal. That right there should let you know how the state feels about you. And the word cell in the dictionary...the only difference is that this cell has electricity! It's hard in here when you don't have nothing, and I don't have shit. I'm looking for someone coming in on the new to fuck over! And to the readers that's in jail, try to get out and don't come back.

Sincerely,
A Dead Man Walking

Eastside Crazy

Terrence Mack
Prisoner Number N95539
Logan Correctional Center
Offense: Murder with Intent to Kill/Injure, Armed Violation, Attempted Murder
Sentence: 60 Years, 30 Years, 30 Years

I appreciate the opportunity that Melvin has given me to write this piece and I hope that my words serve as a warning to you terrorist in the streets. Occasionally, I see your work on the evening news, but I ain't impressed by that shit fool because I did that shit long ago and I have learned some things that you don't know. All that shit that you are choosing to do, will eventually come back on you. This is the inevitable consequences when you fail to use your common sense. So, when the detectives pick you up off the streets and put you in that room where they play hide and seek, don't scream and holler for help because you have no one to blame but yourself. In this room the lights are dim, they can see you, but you can't see all of them. Some are behind a 2-way glass, contemplating how to fame your ass. It matters not that the evidence leads someplace else, because they want you and nobody else. Once you are charged, don't expect your homies to shell out money to help you come home, because most of them are glad that you are gone.

They'll expect your collect calls for awhile, but eventually that will die down and soon the only thing you will hear from the world is that your homies send their love and one of them has your girl. You see, like you I too was loyal to the game. I sacrificed 30 years of my life for representing my gang. I was 16 years old when I caught my offence, the year was 1988, and I haven't been home since. As I sat in the interrogation room with corrupt officials threatening to throw away the key, my homies never sent a lawyer to see about me. I was held on a 10,000 bail and no one ever showed up to bond me out of jail, but the one thing that I will never forget is that they never came to visit to coach me through this shit. I left everyone that really loved me behind, and I don't blame anyone because the choice was mine. I was young and impressionable, and I was tricked to believe that them niggas in the streets really cared about me, but nothing could have been further from the truth. Don't get me wrong, this is not an excuse; I take responsibility for my own actions like a real man should because "out of the worst, the wise will always find some means of good." I have used what I have learned to transform myself, but I can't help but think that I could have learned my lesson someplace else. Over the years, I have lost my mother, grandmother, and other relatives, but I'm counting my blessings because I'm still here. I hope you have learned from what I have been through because if you haven't, I will see you and when you get here, don't try to intrigue me with your stories of the past because I don't give a fuck about what you had and no, I don't have any money to help you start off your bit either. You and your homies never sent me shit, and when you call to the hood and tell the brothers how I treated you, tell them niggas I am waiting on them too.

Eastside Crazy

Dwayne King
Prisoner Number N71761
Lawrence Correctional Center
Offense: Murder with Intent to Kill
Sentence: 44 Years

Supreme Peace Brotha Melvin, I come to you in the name of The God "Born Understanding Allah," a.k.a. Dwayne King/Pus...

After consuming you scribe and digesting the proper nutrients which would enable me to receive a full understanding-I had to pause-re-read the scribe, look again at the name of the sender and just say damn! Never in a million would I've thought that I'll receive a correspondence like this from you...

You've come a long way my brotha and it pleases me to see that you have took a change for the better and the endeavor that you're attempting to achieve is most needed, for our stars (lil brothas) are being extinguished as we speak-"The product of our madness!" so to see that you've awakened from your deaf, dumb, and blind state of mind (i.e., your savage self), and is now trying to bring forth some balance within your universe only shows me that you've become the God (Man) in which you was supposed to be.

Brotha Melvin, I hope you realize that you was that sun that brought forth life upon the planets in which you create (the shorties), and as the two of us have done, we've both created many evil/negative worlds that was captured within our gravitational pull. I hope that I'm not losing you, but for the record, I've made a few changes for the better also. The hood is my foundation and I'll always have love for it. But know this-"Pus is dead!" For I'm now part of a "The Nation of Gods and Earths, a.k.a. The Five Percenters" I Be the God! All my life I brought forth death, violence, and negativity to everything that was within my gravitational pull. I also created evil world, I lived as a Devil and was brainwashed and programmed to cause chaos and confusion towards my own kind (both people and race). But nonetheless, my savage ways/days are over, I'm now on a quest to bring life/positivity to the worlds that I've corrupted in order to bring balance within my universe. Our youths (stars) are our future, and whatever we instill in them is what they'll manifest in life-and as you and I know, "we fucked up!" because the shorties out there are lost, wild and don't give a fuck!

I'm 46 years old and will be 47 in May, when I leave this place, I'll be 64 years old. I've been here since 2002, my outdate is 2027, as I was sentenced to 50 years in prison and must do 25 of it before I get out. I am in here for murder. In a sense, I'm glad I'm locked up because I really don't know who else would have fell victim to my madness. I was also lost and content with the lifestyle that I had chosen, so what you ask of me is something that I must do, not because you asked, but because I owe this to you! You and your generation are the manifestation of the madness that me and my generation produced. We screamed J-M-G, Jeffrey Manor! And held it down with our life-the movement now is La Familia, and you all or should I say your generation held it down with your lives.

For many have died and are doing time! But we must both realize what we've done, because the shorties are out there now following and doing what we taught them. We are the ones that brainwashed and programmed them to do as their doing. We are to blame, but truth be told, you're not? NO! I'm the blame! For I'm the last of my kind, everybody else is dead and who even is out there that's in my age group was influenced by me and my guys, because we was the pace setters and law makers. We considered ourselves the heart of the Manor, and we were spread all the way to what we now call the "back," or better known as the Trumble Park Projects-Blood, sweat, and tears plus many bodies. I remember at one point in time 100 street was the border line. Because we have to fight "nut' and his guys (Fat Jack Father) once we fought our way to 103rd, we had to fight the Latinos from T-P. After that, we took over the projects. I'm talking 77, 78, 79-80 by 85-86, we had everybody screaming J-M-G! Our body count back then was very slim because we was doing all the boding-shit got crazy when we started killing each other. Just a little history for your book, the story must be told. I been planning on writing my memoirs, I just refuse to do it, because I'll be incriminating myself and others, there's too many unsolved cases out there and elsewhere-so I'll partake in what you're doing and help you. You feel me? If you need anything, let me know, but know that I can't say too much for loose lips sink ships!

Melvin, I want you to know and understand that you are a God! For you are the creator of your positive/ good or negative/evil worlds that you create. I once had the concept that you live evil and once

Eastside Crazy

you lived, you went to the Devil because "live" backwards is "evil" and "lived" backwards is "devil." I didn't believe in God and still don't (i.e., the white man's God) because your Heaven or Hell is right here on Earth. It's all what you make out of life. My belief is the Black man is God who is seen and heard everywhere because there's no mysterious spook in the sky!

The Black man is the mystery of life. We are the creators of everything, we're the lost secret, we just don't know it! Once we come to the realization of who we are, as we're doing now, the world will come back to order. It's out of balance because we the Black race don't know who we really are. So it's going to take black men such as yourself and I to bring forth awareness to the youths so they'll know and understand who they really are.

As you can see, all I'm doing is writing whatever comes to mind. I was surprised to hear from you. I just got out of Pontiac SEG, and back amongst the walking dead. I feel out of place because I enjoyed the solitude, had plenty of time to study and reflect on life, my vision has been cleared, and I see life very different now. The blinders been taken off my eyes and what I see, I don't like and it saddens me to know that I was once part of it and a major influence in it. I keep asking myself, why was I left here?

Why didn't I die with my niggas? The only conclusion I keep coming up with is, I must live for them and make it right all the wrong we done in this world, but first I must pay and suffer in this half a bathroom with a bunk in it till I'm 64. For anything else I might go back to my old ways, "Pus" wants his freedom, "Dwain" don't know what to do, but "Born Understanding" is the God that will deliver them all from damnation to paradise...Do you still go back to the land? I heard that "Marty" just came home and "Tootie" is on his way out, what's up with "Jack" I thought he only had to do a eight piece-He should have one foot to the streets too, shouldn't he?

I'm not going to take up too much more of your time. I did enjoy building with you. Stay positive and watch yourself, the bulls eye is on you. Don't let them niggas gain a victory, live for the lost ones!
Peace!
"Born Understanding"
AKA   "PUS"

PS-Send a nigga some flixs...I know you got some, everybody share some!

CIPHER.

Eugene Moore
Prisoner Number 16283-424

Dear Future,

It's always easy to shift the weight and place the blame on others. Sometimes that's what a lot of us do point the finger and shit when all we have to do is look in the mirror. Now point the finger, now place the blame. I could easily place the blame on my mom and dad for bringing me into this world without

Eastside Crazy

having a stable home without having an education. I could easily blame my dad for leaving my mom to raise a man all by herself without a pot to piss in and a window to throw it out, but not me. I'm responsible for my own actions, it's a lot of successful black businessmen out there that was raised by a single parent with no education and moving from house to house but stayed focus and come out on top not me.

I wanted it first, and I wanted the right now, the money and fame I wanted to be like Big Homie, surprise surprise it's me Big Homie don't act like you don't know me. It's a million of me running around this world. I could be your daddy, brother, cuzzin, even your best friend. One thing for sure is if you from the hood you know me. I was that dude that was always on the block. Couldn't hit a block without seeing me. I hustled day and night to get my bread up and let's not forget I kept that iron to get a nigga mind right and if a nigga crossed that line, I didn't waste one minute to put his dick in the dirt. Ain't no peace over east, everybody in the hood wanted to grow up and be like Big Homie, well respected, dress sharp, had all the newest whips, all the bad bitches, his whole team was winning. Big Homie's here to let you know everything that looked good ain't good. I'm here to let you know that's not whats up. Live from the pain and I lived that life live and uncut, you can look me up, I'm now public. When it all comes together Big Homie, just dig a hole he can't get his self out of throwing, all the rocks at the pen basically walking right up to the front gate yelling LET ME IN it's 365 days a year you have to be lucky all of them.

The slick boy just got to catch you slippin once and

it's a wrap you already got a background them nigga that was on the team with you are now on the other team. Witness for the alphabet boys yea yeah they was playing the same game you played, but the feds got the cheat code and them niggas forgot the G code. The feds gave them immunity in exchange for statements on Big Homie. Picture this, the feds tell them you can play for my team and win and score touchdowns or you can play for Big Homie and get a football number, simple math, two plus two, they trade their life for yours. Fuck friends, all the Big Homies of the world got the same story: dead or buried in jail. Once the judge gives you your time, you have been divorced from the streets. Next dude in line to take your place it's a cycle all the bitches that you had that said they love you on a daily is gone and on to the next Big Homie. Game over, all Big Homie got now is a bunch of dreams to be free and federal nightmares and decades away from his family watching his kids grow up, throw pictures, the punishment don't fit the crime, now don't get it fucked up. There is a few dudes in jail without dates they can see, but it's a lot of dudes in jail without dates that say decease but for those who got out dates they can see, I hope they make the best out of a bad situation. It's all kinds of programs you can take and come home with degrees or a trade for those got football #'s and deceased as a out date, P.U.S.H., pray until something happens and keep your head up and hope one day that we were just a sacrifice in the struggle to make the world a better place. Let's make the world a better place. Message from the buried alive, born to die, trying to live. Keep the peace.

Eastside Crazy

Live in the print, Big Jack Herlong, ch.
We all we got.

**Jamilah Taylor
Prisoner Number K67101
Danville Correctional Center
Offense: Murder/Other Forcible Felony
Sentence: 40 Years**

What's up Lil Brotha,
My name is Jamilah Taylor, but those that know me call me Jaymo. I am writing you this letter because of two reasons. One is that the same person that gives a fuck about you gives a fuck about me! Second reason is that I care as well I know that you are saying to yourself, how can you care about me when you don't know me? Well, because I wish that someone that was in the joint could have put me up on what was really going on. I mean, this is not what's happening, for real. I know that you maybe like saying to yourself, dude, you just feel salty because you got caught, but that ain't the case. To keep it 100% real with you if I didn't come to prison, I could have been dead real talk. At that point in my life, I didn't care about nothing. Everybody that I loved died on me. Have you ever seen that movie "Life?" Well, if you have, there's a part in it where Martin is reading a letter to one of his fellow inmates. To make a long story short, the letter said that all of dude's family members were dead. That is a reality for me. When my mother died, I didn't give a fuck about nothing and I wasn't afraid of nothing.

Eastside Crazy

When you have that type of mindset, anything can happen to you, and anyone meaning that you can't think clearly. I wanted to be a gangster, but that shit don't mean nothing when you get popped and come to jail, and you better hope that you don't get no fed case (D.E.A.). They taken all of the stuff from you. Cars, houses, money, everything you got they can take it from you. So you know who the real gangsters are? The Feds are the real gangsters and the U.S. government. Look at how they made everybody move out the projects they took that. So what did all of them dudes who thought they were gangsters do, they let the real gangsters move them out!

Not to sound corny, but Tupac said it best: "you can't keep hitting your fist against a stone wall that's what the white man wants you to do." A Lil Brotha I just want you to open your eyes up just a litl bit more to what's really going on. When I wake up, and walk outside my cell, all I see is faces that look like me, and they ain't the C.O.'s! I hate that I let them enslave me, that's what this is, modern day slavery for real. Lil Brotha, I want you to do two things for me, Ok? One, before you decide to do anything that has a remote chance that you can go to jail/prison for.

I want you to think about all the things that you will be losing: family, girlfriends, cars, clothes, and so called friends. If you think that you got five that will ride or die with you. Think again. When you get locked up, knock that down to just one friend if you are lucky. The girlfriends just like the friends. In fact, she's going to be smashing one of the homies, real talk. The cars you got to sell them for money for the lawyer, they ain't free. And if you want to play with a Public Defender (pretender), you are dead in the water. Family don't have to be there for you just because you got the same D.N.A.. Moms might be there for you if she can, when she can! I just want you to take five seconds to say, is it worth losing my freedom after so many have died before us, just to get it?!

The second thing that I want you to do is to download this rapper called Beanie Sigel. The song is "What Ya Life Like?" It's a good song and it's what my life is like. Signed and seal, my life is real. I just want you to be able to live your life to the fullest. You're 17 man, prom is right around the corner. I had a lot of fun when I went to prom. I wish that I could have went to a real college. I am the first to go to college that I know of in my family, but it's sad that I had to come to prison to do it.

A Lil Brotha want better for yourself and your family.
Your Big Brother on the inside looking out!
Jamilah Taylor
B.K.A. Jaymo